Battleground Europe

NORMANDY

MONT PINÇON

AUGUST 1944

Battleground Europe
NORMANDY

MONT PINÇON

AUGUST 1944

Eric Hunt

LEO COOPER

In memory of Pat Hennessey, the 'young Man in a Tank'

Published by
LEO COOPER
an imprint of
Pen & Sword Books Limited
47 Church Street, Barnsley, South Yorkshire S70 2AS

Copyright © Eric Hunt, 2003

ISBN 0 85052 944 1

A CIP catalogue of this book is available
from the British Library

Printed by Redwood Books Limited
Trowbridge, Wiltshire

*For up-to-date information on other titles produced under the Leo Cooper
imprint, please telephone or write to:*
Pen & Sword Books Ltd, FREEPOST, 47 Church Street
Barnsley, South Yorkshire S70 2AS
Telephone 01226 734222

CONTENTS

ACKNOWLEDGEMENTS

In 1995 I was asked to help with the setting up of a memorial to commemorate all those who served in the 13th/18th Royal Hussars (Queen Mary's Own), from its creation in 1922 to its amalgamation in 1992 with the 15th/19th The King's Royal Hussars – to form The Light Dragoons. The previous year had been the fiftieth anniversary of the D Day landings in Normandy, and an obvious site for the memorial was Mont Pinçon. In August 1944 the Regiment had played a signal part in the capture of this important feature. The preparations for the memorial and its dedication led me to research the details of the operation and from that developed a range of happy contacts with a number of people, both from the other units that took part and the local village of le Plessis Grimoult.

The *Journal of The Society for Army Historical Research* subsequently published an article by me on *The Battle for Mont Pinçon* and in 1998 Adrian Gregory, who had also served in the 13th/18th, produced the video *Battle for Mont Pinçon 5th, 6th and 7th August 1944.* That included a number of interviews with veterans of the 43rd Division and the 13/18 Hussars as well as inhabitants of le Plessis Grimoult and Adrian has kindly allowed me to make use of them. I am also most grateful to those he interviewed; they are listed below (under regiments and ranks at the time of the battle). Several of them, alas, have since died (marked†).

13th/18th Royal Hussars: Cpl Roy Cadogan, Lt Hugh Elliot, Capt Julius Neave, Major Sir Delaval Cotter†, Lt Hugh Franks, Tpr George Treloar, Lt Brian Edwards, L/Cpl Pat Hennessey†, Tpr Douglas Wileman.
Royal Artillery: Capt David Hadow, Sgt Jim Parkins.
Royal Hampshire Regiment: L/Cpl Ken Baker, CSM Laurie Symes.
Duke of Cornwall's Light Infantry: Sgt Fred Bolt, Pte James Gregory†.
Wiltshire Regiment: L/Cpl Ron Garner, Pte Will Hanson, Capt Tom Powell, Capt Harry Peace†, Major 'Dim' Robbins, Cpl Neville Trim.
Somerset Light Infantry: Lt Sydney Jary, Cpl Douglas Proctor†.
Inhabitants of le Plessis Grimoult: Mme Jeanne Groult, M. le Marchand, Mme Madeleine Restout†.

My other sources for this short book range from Chester Wilmot's *The Struggle for Europe,* through formation and regimental histories and war diaries, to personal accounts by 'those who were there'. Of these last, some date from after the events described to reminiscences fifty years or more on. It may seem that the more immediate the recollection, the more valuable for those of us who want to walk the battlefield. Personally, I think that they all have a place – as have fresh young wines and those of distinguished vintage! I am indebted to all those on whose recollections I have drawn, amongst whom were 'Dim' Robbins and

David Hadow, who were also kind enough to let me have comments on an early draft. So too did the late Pat Hennessey, who must have been one of the youngest British tank commanders in Normandy. Adrian Gregory has not only let me quote liberally from his video, but has provided a mass of supporting material from his own researches.

Thanks are also due to: David Fletcher, The Tank Museum; The Air Photo Library, University of Keele; The National Army Museum, Imperial War Museum, Robert Hale Ltd (*Normandy Diary* Lord Methuen); Harper Collins Publishers Ltd (*Struggle for Europe* Chester Wilmot). Ralph Dodds and my wife Gill have undertaken the scanning of various drafts and, finally, Roni Wilkinson of Pen & Sword Books has worked wonders in finding pictures and matching them to text.

EEH, *Mappowder, July 2003*

Single track roads, numerous fields bordered by banking, ditches and high hedges made up the terrain over which Operation BLUECOAT was fought.

INTRODUCTION

Of all the local actions which shaped the pattern of the break-out battle, the attack upon Mont Pinçon was one of the most significant, not merely on account of its tactical consequences, but because of the qualities which it called forth in the men concerned.

STRUGGLE FOR EUROPE

One hundred days after D Day – on Thursday 14 September 1944 – the main story on the front page of the *Daily Mail* had news of sweeping successes by the Allied armies which were 'closing in' on Germany. American troops had captured their first German village and the British Second Army had pushed the Germans off their line on the Albert Canal. On the same page a 'local action' was reported from some six weeks earlier:

This Was the Epic of Mont Pinçon
'Red Rose' Colonel and His Heroes

Mont Pinçon, 1,200ft, highest point in Normandy, lay between Caen and the British advance on the Seine. It was in German hands, and from it enemy fire paralysed all movement over miles of country.

The 43rd Wessex Division, pinned down for seven hours on end, were given the order to attack.

A colonel, wearing a red rose on his battledress and swinging a cane, led his men forward, strolling casually over a bridge under heavy machine gun fire.

His men, spurred on, took the bridge and the hill. The full story of the action – one of the most crucial of the Normandy battle – is told today.

Throughout the whole advance in the west it has been the lot of our Allies to sweep across three countries, dragging the headlines with them. This story tells of the men who made those headlines possible ...

The men who made that particular headline possible came from 43rd Wessex Division and 8 Independent Armoured Brigade, together with those fighting alongside them from the other formations of XXX Corps – 50th Northumbrian and 7th Armoured Divisions – and those of VIII Corps – Guards and 11th Armoured Divisions, 15th Scottish Division and 6 Guards

Independent Tank Brigade. They were all taking part in Operation BLUECOAT, launched on 30 July 1944, which saw some of the fiercest fighting of the Normandy campaign over an area some ten miles wide and twelve miles deep.

This guide is concerned principally with the capture of the key feature of Mont Pinçon; it therefore follows 43rd Division and 8 Armoured Brigade, from their assembly area near Caumont-l'Éventé, into the *bocage* and up the slopes of Mont Pinçon. But the stories of the other formations are also outlined, as the Mont Pinçon story is best understood by keeping track of the other actions of BLUECOAT.

OUTLINE OF GUIDE

Chapter 1 – Operations COBRA and BLUECOAT
The break out from the bridgehead begins with the successful launch of the American Operation COBRA and plans for a supporting offensive by British Second Army are brought forward. Three armoured and two infantry divisions, with additional armoured and infantry brigades, are to be launched in Operation BLUECOAT. There has to be speedy and complex regrouping in the British sector of the bridgehead.

Chapter 2 – 30 & 31 July: XXX Corps
43rd and 50th Divisions encounter tough resistance and make slow progress through the *bocage*, but eventually 43rd Division reach St Pierre-du-Fresne after taking Briquessard and Cahagnes and 50th Division reach the Launay feature.

Chapter 3 – 30 & 31 July: VIII Corps
15th Division get on much better than 43rd and 50th, but find themselves in a very exposed position, as XXX Corps cannot cover their left flank at Quarry Hill. 11th Armoured do well on the right, reaching the outskirts of St Martin-des-Besaces and taking an unobserved bridge over the River Souleuvre. First news arrives of German panzer reinforcements as Guards Armoured Division moves forward.

Chapter 4 – 1 & 2 August: XXX Corps
7th Armoured Division is brought in on the left flank, heading for Aunay-s-Odon, while the two infantry divisions

9

slog on towards Villers-Bocage and Ondefontaine. 43rd Division reaches the Bois du Homme and takes Jurques and le Bigne. 50th Division secures the Launay feature and takes Amayé-sur-Seulles and la Bruyère. The lack of progress by the Corps is unacceptable and a number of senior officers are replaced.

Chapter 5 – 1 & 2 August: VIII Corps

German counter-attacks are launched against 15th Division and Guards Armoured Division, moving up through them, meets heavy opposition. However, 11th Armoured forges on beyond the Caen-Vire road. 3rd Division joins the Corps to help hold on to the ground won and maintain the forward impetus.

Chapter 6 – 3 & 4 August: XXX Corps

43rd Division clears Jurques on the 3rd and Ondefontaine on the 4th. Counter attacks hold up 7th Armoured, but they by-pass Aunay-sur-Odon and secure the high ground beyond, while their armoured cars reach the outskirts of Villers-Bocage, occupied by 50th Division on the 4th.

Chapter 7 – 3 & 4 August: VIII Corps

Both 11th Armoured and Guards Armoured Divisions are being subjected to heavy German counter-attacks by the panzer divisions brought across from the eastern sector of the Normandy battlefields. 15th Division is able to advance eastward to clear the ridge towards Montchauvet.

Chapter 8 – 5 August: 'Converging on Mont Pinçon'

The first assault on the defences of Mont Pinçon itself, by 129 Brigade and two squadrons of the 13/18 Hussars, is held up at St Jean-le-Blanc and la Varinière.

Chapters 9 – 6 August: 'A footing'

129 Brigade's second assault, together with a feint attack by 130 Brigade gains the lower slopes of Mont Pinçon.

Chapters 10 – Evening of 6 August: The Assault

In the early evening, two troops of the 13/18 Hussars find an unwatched track up the hill and reach the summit. The remainder of A Squadron join them together with Regimental Headquarters and then B Squadron. Two of the exhausted battalions of the Brigade, 4 Som LI and 4 Wiltshire, follow them up as a heavy mist and darkness fall.

Chapter 11 – Elsewhere on 5 & 6 August
7th Armoured Division enters Aunay-sur-Odon and pushes on towards Thury Harcourt. VIII Corps spends much of 5 August mopping up enemy pockets and preparing for renewed counter-attacks. They arrive with great intensity on 6 August from Vire to Mont Pinçon.

Chapter 12 – 6/7 August: Night on Mont Pinçon and in la Varinière
The much-depleted 5 Wiltshire, with C Squadron 13th/18th, hold on to la Varinière while British and German troops share the summit of Mont Pinçon. 214 Brigade is ordered forward to clear the Mont Pinçon feature and capture le Plessis Grimoult. French civilians are caught up in the battle.

Chapter 13 – 7 August: Capture of le Plessis Grimoult
5 DCLI and B Squadron 4/7 Dragoon Guards capture le Plessis Grimoult.

Chapter 14 – After the capture of Mont Pinçon:
The next few days – A month later – Battle Honours

Mont Pinçon

Mont Pinçon, the highest feature in Normandy, rises some 1,200 feet from the *pré-bocage* on the edge of the *bocage* proper. In 1939 the French positioned on it a navigation aid (*station de radionavigation*, predecessor to radar), which was subsequently taken over by the Luftwaffe and used in directing air raids on England.

The Germans also identified Mont Pinçon as a main feature

Mount Pinçon in 2003.

of an inland defence line early in the Normandy campaign. At that stage, Allied deception plans had convinced the enemy that further landings were possible and a strong probability was the coast north of the Seine. Eleven days after D Day, at a briefing at Hitler's French command post, the Commander-in-Chief West, Field Marshal von Rundstedt, had warned that Allied air power and naval artillery were such that he was unable to attack the Normandy bridgehead with any hope of success. With him was Commander Army Group B, Field Marshal Rommel, and he proposed a gradual withdrawal to a defensive line, beyond the reach of the naval guns, from which the panzer formations would be free to operate against either any breakout from the bridgehead or a fresh landing. The new line would follow the River Orne south to Thury-Harcourt and then turn west to Mont Pinçon and follow the range of hills westward to the coast near Granville.

Hitler rejected Rommel's proposal and it was several weeks before Mont Pinçon featured in the campaign.

The *Bocage*

Operation BLUECOAT was fought in progressively more hilly country, broken by streams flowing through steep-sided valleys. The hills were covered with thick woodland while the characteristic dairy farms and orchards of the region occupied the valleys and slopes. The small fields and innumerable, often sunken, side-roads were lined with banked hedgerows and ditches. Stone walls enclosed the orchards and the stone buildings and narrow streets of the villages completed a countryside ideal for the defenders. For their infantry there were any number of natural anti-tank obstacles while their tanks found ample cover in the thick woods and copses. But the attacker:

> ...was forced to follow by-ways which straggle up and down against the contours. These by-ways were mostly sunken lanes, so narrow that a tank could not traverse its gun, still less turn round. There was no observation beyond the next field and the armour was seldom able to manoeuvre across country, for the hedgerows were effective barriers and any gaps could easily be closed with mines and fire. The bocage was made for the sniper and the man who lay in wait beside the road with a panzerfaust.

In 1991, Bobby Neave, second-in-command of B Squadron 13/18 Hussars remembered:

Caught in the open these German Tigers manoeuvre frantically to avoid Allied fighter bombers in the fields and hedges of the *bocage*.

...very enclosed country, leafy hedges, narrow roads, totally unsuitable for tank operations... you advanced across a field and the next thing you knew you were being attacked by panzerfaust from behind; a unit of the other side sitting comfortably in the corner behind a high bank... not easy fighting.

Men of Wessex

The Wyvern, badge of the fighting men of Wessex, had been the formation sign of 43rd (Wessex) Division since 1935. When the division came ashore in Normandy between 23 and 24 June 1944 it was still composed largely of West Country units. They had been commanded since 1942 by Major General G. I. Thomas, 'a very tough and often brutal martinet with a professional, almost Teutonic, attitude to divisional command.' During their training in south-east Kent over three winters:

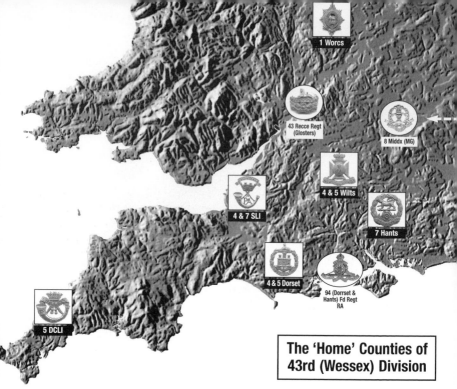

**The 'Home' Counties of
43rd (Wessex) Division**

*. . . the Division grew to accept hardship as the natural order
of things. By a lucky chance, also, the enclosed country round
Stone Street strikingly resembled the Normandy bocage . . . the
Division, in contrast to those accustomed only to the limitless
open spaces of the Western Desert, became particularly well
attuned to the conditions it had to face from the very moment it
landed in France.*

Two days after landing they were in action outside Caen as part
of VIII Corps. Between 25 and 29 June they took part in VIII
Corps' Odon offensive, in which 15th (Scottish) Division and
they were to seize and secure a bridgehead across the River
Odon, from which 11th Armoured Division could attack south-
east. This drew the German reserves into the Caen sector and at
one stage three panzer divisions were attacking 43rd Division
alone. Meanwhile Caen had yet to be captured and I Corps, after
a devastating attack by Bomber Command, finally achieved that
on 9 July.

Then came the operation to secure the high ground between
the rivers Odon and Orne. Two armoured brigades and an extra
infantry brigade, together with the guns of two army group RAs

and two other divisions, supported 43rd Division. The ferocious battle over the next two days left the division with over 2,000 casualties and was followed by fourteen days of 'conditions comparable to the bombardment at Passchendaele'. 6 [A full account is in *Hill 112, Battles of the Odon* in the Battleground Europe series.]

The casualties included a high proportion of commanding officers and company commanders. The replacements, officers and men, had only a few days to settle in with the survivors during a brief spell in a rest area at Ducy-Ste-Marguerite, before the division was committed to its next operation. They had hoped to have seven to ten days in reserve, but events were moving too swiftly for that hope to be fulfilled.

Amongst the replacements was Lieutenant Sydney Jary of the Hampshire Regiment. In the event he was posted to 4 Somerset Light Infantry which, in two days, had been almost decimated. Jary was one of fifteen officers and nearly 550 other ranks who joined what had been a close-knit, 'family' unit. He had had previous experience of 6-pounder anti-tank guns and was posted as second-in-command to the battalion's Anti-Tank Platoon.

Amphibious Cavalry

Tanks of eight armoured regiments of the British, American and Canadian assault forces had been equipped for amphibious landing on D Day. Three of the eight were now in 8 Independent Armoured Brigade: the 4/7 Dragoon Guards, the 13/18 Royal Hussars and the Nottinghamshire (Sherwood Rangers) Yeomanry. The 'DD' (= duplex drive) regiments had varied fortunes on D Day, but the 13th/18th had been the most successful in getting tanks of its two DD squadrons ashore. Then in 27 Armoured Brigade, part of I Corps then among the first to land on Sword Beach, the 13th/18th 'swam' their amphibious Sherman tanks nearly five thousand yards in heavy seas. By the second half of July they had had a full share of the subsequent fighting. I Corps was and securing the left flank of VIII Corps during the seven-day battle of Operation GOODWOOD – the attempt by three armoured divisions to break out from the beachhead. On the evening of 26 July, 27 Armoured Brigade was ordered into army reserve at Coulombs, not far from the 43rd Division rest area. There they were

Sherman DD (duplex drive) tank with floatation skirt folded.

dismayed to hear that they were to take down their 'Sea-horse' formation sign. 27 Brigade was being disbanded and the 13th/18th were to replace the 24th Lancers and wear the 'Fox's Mask' of 8 Independent Armoured Brigade.

8 Armoured Brigade had played the same part for XXX Corps during D Day as had 27 Brigade for I Corps, but conditions had not permitted their DD tanks to be launched and they had to be beached from the tank landing craft which had brought them across the Channel. Also in the Brigade were a motor battalion, the 12/60 (Queen's Westminster) King's Royal Rifle Corps and 147 Field Regiment RA (Essex Yeomanry). Earlier in the month they had been supporting 50th (Northumbrian) Division in a bloody attack on Hottot where they had encountered the *bocage* for the first time. They then relieved 2nd (US) Armoured Division north-east of Caumont-l'Eventé and had remained static for the remainder of the month occupying that section of the beachhead perimeter.

Men and Weapons

Veterans of 43rd Division and 8 Armoured Brigade interviewed by Adrian Gregory recalled the quality of the German soldier and the effectiveness of his weapons, compared with their own:

THE WARRANT OFFICERS

Major 'Dim' Robbins, company commander in 4 Wiltshire:

When we captured a German position we frequently found it had been commanded by a warrant officer. When asked why? 'The officers have gone back to reconnoitre the next position and we are quite capable of commanding a company. I thought they were.

SS troops manning a M-42 machine gun.

MACHINE GUNS

Lieutenant Sydney Jary:

The Germans understood the use of suppressive firepower far better than we did. We had been trained on the Bren light machine gun which fired at the rate of about 450 rounds per minute and it was magazine fed. The German MG 42 was belt fed and fired at a rate of 1200 rounds per minute. Many of the German sections were armed with two of these weapons.

Lance Corporal Ken Baker, of 7 Hampshire:

Where the Bren would gain was that it was an accurate weapon. You could knock somebody's eye out with it at a hundred yards without any difficulty. The German gun was more like a hosepipe and when the Germans used machine guns, it was guns rather than gun. There might be half a dozen of them; invariably they supported one another. The general cross-fire from them was virtually impossible to get through.

MORTARS
Ken Baker:
You have to bear in mind that the Germans were basically retreating, slowly, but retreating. They had all the positions and all the distances taped – to the metre. You would get to a cross roads and it suddenly rained mortar shells. Without your getting away from those cross roads there was no way of surviving at all. They would come over in clouds, absolute clouds.
NEBELWERFER

German paratroopers, *Fallschirmjäger*, operating the 8.1cm 34 mortar. This posed photograph supposedly shows the bomb in process of leaving the barrel. It would be a foolhardy cameraman who stood in this position during actual firing.

The *Nebelwerfer* six-barrelled mortar.

Sydney Jary:

> The Germans also had a nebelwerfer; a multi barrelled weapon. When it fired it made a ghastly noise like a cow retching.

Private Will Hanson of 5 Wiltshires:

> Terrible, terrible... called the 'Moaning Minnie'. ... Those things went creaming up ... they didn't do a terrible lot if you could get down ... you were safe, but they made such a terrifying noise they frightened you.

Captain David Hadow, 94 Field Regiment Royal Artillery

> The rocket propelled Moaning Minnie could be fired and out of action and on the move before the rounds landed. This made it very difficult to engage them.

SHERMAN TANKS V GERMAN 88MM GUNS

Lieutenant Hugh Elliot, troop leader in 13/18 Hussars:

> Everyone using the diesel Sherman tank realised its shortcomings but we had a great affinity for it because it was such an incredibly reliable tank; it hardly ever broke down. ...You were aware that you were very thin-skinned so far as the 88 was

A German 88 mm gun operating in the anti-tank role.

concerned or even German 75s – long barrelled 75s. They penetrated very easily, even at the front. So we did have spaced armour fitted to most of our tanks on the front but this was probably more psychological armour than anything else! But our 75 was a good gun, very good HE performance; the AP performance was a bit pathetic unless you were fairly close to. But the [Browning] machine guns were brilliant. So, as an infantry support tank, the Sherman was very good indeed.

Corporal Roy Cadogan, 13/18 Hussars:

Terrible, frightening – absolutely frightening. I was hit later on; I was knocked out by what I believe was a German 88 went into the side of my tank; it fired three shells. We all managed to get out; I was the troop leader's operator at the time. He and the gunner got out first and by the time I was out it was well and truly on fire.

Lance Corporal Pat Hennessey, 13/18 Hussars:

The shortcomings of the Sherman tank were quite serious. First of all the armour plating compared with that of a German Tiger tank: there was practically no comparison. The front of the Sherman was considerably less armoured than the frontal armour of a Tiger. The result was that an 88 mm gun mounted on a Tiger tank could go through a Sherman like a knife through butter. Whereas our 75 mm would hit a Tiger and you would see the tracer bounce straight up in the air and they would just bounce off the top. ...A disconcerting thing about the Sherman was its propensity to burst into flames and this they did with monotonous regularity. Every time a Sherman was hit nine times out of ten it would catch fire, in a most horrific fashion.

> *So, from the technical point of view we were out gunned when face to face with a German tank. Nevertheless, we did have our successes, which must say a lot for of our training, the morale of our troops and the quite excellent leadership we enjoyed.*

(Pat Hennessey had joined up in 1941 at the age of sixteen, having given his age as eighteen – at the prompting of the recruiting sergeant. In June 1945 Hennessey, now a sergeant went to the RAC OCTU and was commissioned in 1946. He transferred to the RAF in 1951, in which he reached the rank of Group Captain. His wartime memoirs *Young Man in a Tank* were privately published in 1988.)

AIR SUPREMACY

Pat Hennessey wrote:

> *We certainly felt the lack of air cover when the weather precluded flying operations at the time of the great storm just after the landings. ... Our advance would have been much more difficult, if not impossible, had we not had air supremacy. Weather permitting, the Royal Air Force provided almost constant air cover, so that any movement by the enemy in daylight attracted immediate response from the RAF's fighter bombers. They did a magnificent job on our behalf, and on one occasion we were given the chance to see how it felt from the Germans' point of view. We were in a clearing near a wood when we saw a section of two aircraft circling in the sky. Suddenly, to our horror, they dived on us with cannon and machine guns firing. I hastily threw out the yellow smoke aircraft recognition canisters, and frantically waved the large yellow silk recognition panels we had for just such an event.*
>
> *Fortunately, they must have seen our signals, because they stopped their attack and flew away. No damage had been done, but we thought ourselves lucky that they were not using their tank busting rockets; they were Spitfires, not Typhoons. Nevertheless, it had been a very near thing. No doubt it is difficult to tell one type of tank from another from the cockpit of a fast moving aircraft, but we could not help wishing that the airmen would become a little more expert at it.*

Several accounts tell of problems with close air support during BLUECOAT; the *bocage* added to the problems of identifying friend from foe. 11th Armoured Division, operating on the

21

immediate left of the American sector had several unfortunate experiences from American Thunderbolts, which were 'notoriously trigger-happy':

They swarmed over the thin red line of the British defences and bombed everyone in sight despite the orange phosphorescent panels displayed on the top of the Fife and Forfar Shermans at Pavée and yellow smoke emitted by special smoke generators.

Nearby at La Biste, Corporal Reg Worton of 1st Herefords remembers:

Our carriers were parked all round the sides of a field when a Yankee Thunderbolt came snooping round at hedge height and you could see the pilot. A Jerry gun shot at him which scared him and he sliced right down my section and hit [Private] Wilf Finnikin, one of my drivers, who died in my arms.

Another Thunderbolt attacked an 8 RB First Aid Post at Presles, which had a plainly visible Red Cross, and discharged all its rockets. Fortunately only the trucks were hit.

However Rifleman Roland Jefferson was impressed with the RAF Typhoon support: 'More often than not when they appeared they would score for us.'

HARBOURING/LEAGUERING

In the accounts of armoured regiment operations there are a number of references to 'harbours' or 'leaguers'. Before the days of night vision devices, tanks were 'blind' after dark and particularly vulnerable to infantry attack. One reason for harbouring or leaguering was therefore to provide for better protection and, if no friendly infantry were securing the area, tank crewmen stood watch with small arms and machine guns dismounted from the tanks. But the harbours also provided the rendezvous with the A Echelons, carrying fuel, ammunition and rations and, as the historian of 4/7 Royal Dragoon Guards commented:

If the cavalry soldier of the old days had been beset with all the laborious chores of horse-management in the field, his armoured successor was even more burdened. As darkness closed in after a hard day's action the squadrons would be pulled back to harbour positions where the crews could at last clamber out, stiff, hungry and weary. But there was no rest until the essential tasks of 'tanking up', 'bombing up' and general maintenance had been completed. The weighty 75mm or 17pdr rounds had to be manhandled up through the turret hatches and stowed in the

Republic P-47C Thunderbolt.

Scramble! A British pilot races to his Typhoon fighter. British ground troops were happier when they were receiving support from British squadrons.

British tank crews resting up for the night.

turret bins; Browning belts filled and likewise stowed; dozens of 4½-gallon jerricans to be heaved on to the engine deck and emptied into fuel tanks; engines and guns to be checked, cleaned, oiled. Then there was the perpetual 'track bashing' – checking for damaged track-pins, adjustment of tension. The crews were lucky if they could bed down under their tanks by midnight. Even then, members would have to do their stint of wireless watch in the turret, crackling headset and occasional chatter helping to fight off sleep. Usually engines would roar into life by 0430 hours, Troop and Squadron wirelesses would be netted in, and by first light the column of tanks would roll forth to marry up with their trudging 'Feet'.

Chapter One

Operations COBRA and BLUECOAT

The Break-Out Begins

The Allied strategy had brought the principal German strength against the British and Canadian forces at the eastern end of the Normandy bridgehead. Their Seventh Army was then unable to resist the American offensive on 25 July, when First US Army under General Omar Bradley thrust due south from St Lô in Operation COBRA. General Montgomery anticipated that the effect on the Germans of COBRA would be to 'bend back' their line and that they would try to stabilise it on three 'strong hinges': at Caumont-l'Éventé, on the Orne and on the high ground between Caen and Falaise. On the day that COBRA was launched, at the other end of the bridgehead, the Germans repulsed a Canadian attack at Bourguebus Ridge, inflicting heavy casualties. However, the attack kept Panzer Group West fully engaged and it was another two days before

American breakthrough during Operation COBRA. Here an American column is driving towards Coutances.

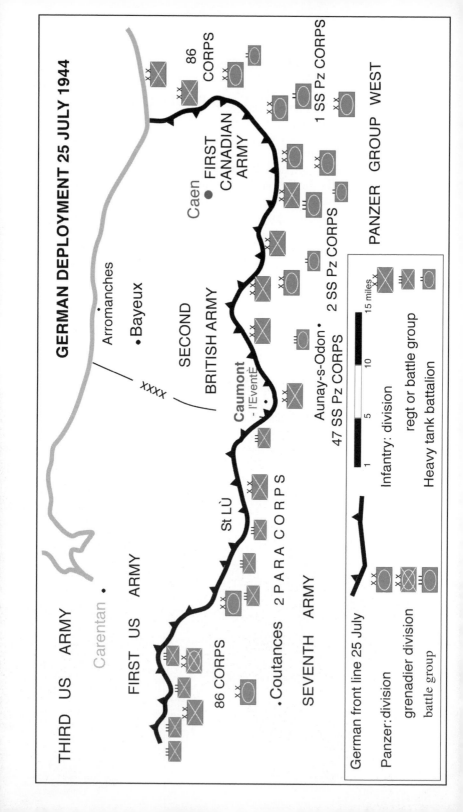

GERMAN DEPLOYMENT 25 JULY 1944

THIRD US ARMY

FIRST US ARMY

86 CORPS

Carentan

Coutances

SEVENTH ARMY

St LÙ

2 PARA CORPS

Caumont
l'Eventè

SECOND
BRITISH ARMY

Bayeux

Arromanches

Caen

FIRST CANADIAN
ARMY

86
CORPS

1 SS Pz CORPS

PANZER GROUP WEST

2 SS Pz CORPS

Aunay-s-Odon

47 SS Pz CORPS

German front line 25 July

Panzer: division

grenadier division

battle group

Infantry: division

regt or battle group

Heavy tank battalion

1   5   10   15 miles

Feldmarschäll von Kluge (who had replaced von Rundstedt as Commander-in-Chief West) could spare any of its armour to reinforce the German Seventh Army. Then two panzer divisions, 2nd and 17th, were sent off on a forced march from the Orne to the Vire. By the time they could get there, under continuous attack from the air, the Americans were making such good progress that an operation in support of their offensive by Second British Army was brought forward.

General Mongomery's plan was for Second British Army to 'knock out the key rivets in the north'. The Army Commander, General Dempsey, was

Feldmarschäll von Kluge.

An advanced aid post in use by *Fallschirmjäger* and SS troops.

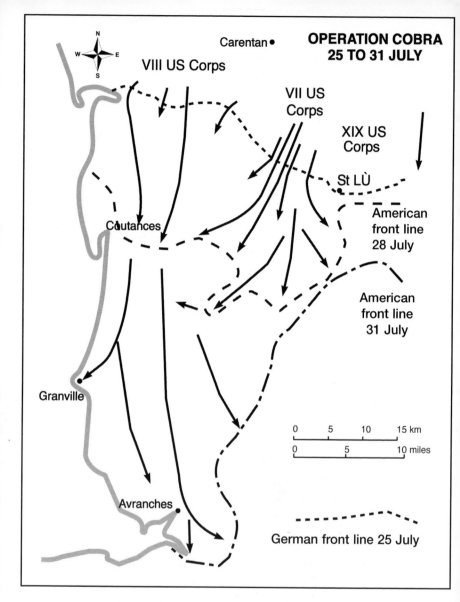

Carentan •

OPERATION COBRA
25 TO 31 JULY

VIII US Corps

VII US Corps

XIX US Corps

St LÙ

American front line 28 July

Coutances

American front line 31 July

Granville

0   5   10   15 km
0   5   10 miles

Avranches

German front line 25 July

therefore planning to attack on 2 August with VIII Corps from Caumont, but the rapid American advance and the movement of German armour westward made it essential that Second Army should strike without delay. On 28 July, Montgomery ordered a rapid transfer of Dempsey's armour to the Caumont area in order to mount an attack on 30 July by both VIII and XXX Corps – Operation BLUECOAT.

On the right flank of Second Army, V (US) Corps was advancing on Torigni-sur-Vire against strong German resistance. The British boundary with them followed the line of the River Drôme. On 29 July the enemy opposite VIII and XXX Corps was believed to be the 326th, 276th and 277th Infantry Divisions – the German armour was all farther east in the Orne sector where there were six panzer and SS panzer divisions.

The plan for Operation BLUECOAT was for XXX Corps to push south-east, to the line Villers-Bocage – Aunay-sur-Odon, while VIII Corps, in a wider sweep on its right, swung down to the general area St Martin-des-Besaces – le Bény Bocage – Forêt l'Éveque, and on to the triangle formed by Vire, Tinchebray and Condé-sur-Noireau. The whole area was more hilly and wooded than the country in the bridgehead and the principal feature was a series of hills running south-east between le Bény Bocage and Aunay-sur-Odon. Some of the hills were over 1,000 feet high and the highest was Mont Pinçon. It was the most rugged part of the *bocage* and the enemy was strongly entrenched on the slopes and ridges. They had had plenty of time to lay extensive minefields – and there were not only German minefields to be dealt with. The area over which BLUECOAT was to be launched had been static for several weeks and both the British and the Americans had laid minefields of which there was little or no record.

Amongst the German defensive positions, at the western end of the Mont Pinçon range, were 'Hill 361' and 'Hill 309'. By seizing them and exploiting towards Vire, Montgomery hoped, not only to cover part of Bradley's flank and deprive the Germans of their 'hinge', but also to thrust in behind the new front which German Seventh Army was forming along the River Vire. Here there was no sign of enemy withdrawal; V (US) Corps had been attacking strongly since the 26th, but had been able to drive the Germans only a few miles back.

Regrouping

Before Operation BLUECOAT could begin there had to be substantial and difficult regrouping. An armoured division had over 3,400 vehicles and, in order to get into position near Caumont, those of 11th and Guards Armoured had to cross from one side of the British sector to the other, right across the supply lines of both XII and XXX Corps. Twenty-one miles of roads, many of them specially made by Corps Pioneers, speedily became heavily cut up, congested and dusty. But, as could now be taken for granted, the Military Police achieved wonders in keeping the traffic moving. Montgomery wrote later: 'This movement was a major undertaking and Second Army organised it beautifully.'

On 26 July, 43rd Division had handed over 'the battle scarred slopes of Hill 112 and the stinking ruins of Maltot' to another division and moved back to Ducy-Ste-Marguerite, south-east of Bayeux. From there they enjoyed the luxury of a bath and clean underwear at the RAOC's Mobile Laundry and Bath Unit while urgent steps were taken to reequip the division's units and bring them back to strength. The urgency was fully justified. Unexpected orders to move reached units during the night of 28/29 July and the division was on the march the following day.

On 28 July the 13/18 Hussars, like the units of 43rd Division, had been enjoying what had been promised as a seven-day 'rest' at Coulombs. The remaining DD tanks of A and B Squadrons were being replaced from those of the departing Staffordshire Yeomanry and all the tanks had been stripped down and the ammunition unstowed. Captain Bobby Neave, second-in-command of B Squadron, later remembered the brief respite as providing a 'pleasant two or three days, to change badges on our tanks and uniforms and sample the calvados' before fighting in the *bocage*.

Captain Julius Neave, Adjutant 13th/18th Royal Hussars.

Julius Neave, the Adjutant of the 13th/18th and Bobby's brother, was keeping an unofficial diary:

'Before D Day it had not occurred to me to that I might keep a diary (In fact the keeping of diaries on active service was not allowed and being aware of this undoubtedly influenced what I recorded), but finding after arrival on the other side that I had jotted some notes on an

'Monty is determined to make us catch up on the Yanks who are doing magnificently'. GIs fighting in the *bocage*.

Engagement Block it seemed a good scheme to keep it going, so I took to writing up the day's events in an 'S.O. Book 136'.

On the 28th he was woken by his batman with news of a warning order for the regiment to be ready to move at noon the following day. He was not best pleased:

'Perfectly ridiculous and nonsensical having been given a week to reorganise in. Steamed off to Brigade after breakfast; found the Brigadier [GE Prior Palmer] ... in a towering rage and just tearing off to 2nd Army and 30 Corps to sort it all out ... The uncertainty and lack of decision about the immediate future is most unsettling. Having laid on a very comprehensive programme of refitting and reorganisation and giving everyone a jerk to get cracking before joining 8th Armoured Brigade, it's disheartening to find that once again we are in the buggery stakes ...

'The next bombshell came that we were to move at 0600 tomorrow – getting worse – conference called and laid on the rough plan. Obviously it will be a fair shambles but it can't be helped. No sooner had the conference ended than messages arrived to say we were to move during the night so as to arrive by daylight. ...

'Tear off to Brigade to get the form and learn that Monty is determined to make us catch up on the Yanks who are doing magnificently – the only difference between us is (a) that their army is twice as big and (b) that we have double the opposition against us.'

He found that 8 Armoured Brigade was joining XXX Corps, and, for the first phase of the new operation, was to be in support of 43rd Division, less 13/18 Hussars who were to support 50th Division.

On the 29th, Julius Neave wrote:

'We didn't move during the night of course, having packed up, but left at 0600. Colonel and I broke off half-way to call at 50 Division who said we were going to the wrong place, so rerouted the Regiment on the line of march, we harboured in an orchard west of Tilly and south of Bayeux in the 'Cream of the Bocage country.' What 'Bocage' means, God knows, but to 2nd Army it means almost jungle country, it's so thick. Stuffed with orchards and grass fields all about 100 yards square and with gunners and spandaus, mortars, mines, booby traps and other troubles in every hedgerow it is also the bazooka's paradise.

British troops moving up to the start line.

'A typical pre-battle day of conferences and coming and going. More difficult than usual this time as we are in a new Brigade working with a new Division and have no codes or form, and have Squadrons split up to Brigades and troops to Battalions. Also we were yesterday at this time fondly oblivious of war and having all tanks and vehicles in little bits and pieces.

'Traffic on the roads beyond belief. 50 Division ... are, however, tired and below strength. They are now 60% reinforcements and have no D-Day Battalion Commander left and only very few Company or Platoon Commanders.'

The 13th/18th had lost their own D Day Commanding Officer, Lieutenant Colonel Dick Harrap, on 16 June and were now commanded by Lieutenant Colonel Vincent Dunkerly. He had come across from the 23 Hussars where he had been a squadron leader.

A Sherman with spare track links and wheels carried at the front as extra armour.

Chapter Two

30 and 31 July – XXX Corps

For XXX Corps, Operation BLUECOAT began at 0600 hours 30 July. 43rd Division was to secure the hill feature about Point 361 to the west of Jurques, while 50th Division on its left was to secure the high ground west and north-west of Villers-Bocage.

Briquessard, Cahagnes and St Pierre-du-Fresne
43rd Division
In the centre of the BLUECOAT attack, 43rd Division's first task was to force through enemy positions at Briquessard and

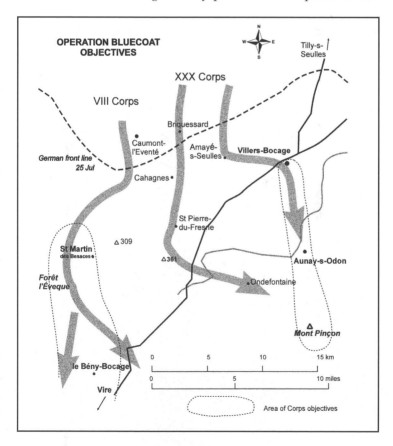

Somerset Light Infantry.

north of Cahagnes and advance via St Pierre-du-Fresne to seize Bois du Homme (or Bois de Brimbois) – the high ground west and south-west of Jurques. At the same time they were to protect the eastern flank of XXX Corps by seizing and holding the la Bigne feature. Finally, they were to swing east and capture the high ground at Ondefontaine as a base for further deep reconnaissance in easterly and south-easterly direction. 130 Brigade, augmented by 4 Somerset Light Infantry, was to lead the assault. Once they had penetrated the German line, 214 Brigade was to pass through and advance to St Pierre-du-Fresne; from there 129 Brigade could tackle the Bois du Homme. But, the division had a discouraging start when the battle began in their sector at 0800 hrs on 30 July.

130 Brigade

A dense minefield and a steep-sided stream, impassable to tanks, confronted the two leading companies of 4 Somerset Light Infantry on the left, advancing on Briquessard astride a narrow country lane. They suffered many casualties from *schuh* mines scattered in the neighbouring fields and the road too was mined, along which the supporting tanks from B Squadron Sherwood Rangers were trying to move. But there was one stroke of luck; an Allied bomber flying very low dropped several bombs on the northern edge of Briquessard and the Som

German Teller mine.

German schuh mine showing the amount of ball bearings contained in each mine.

LI were quick to take advantage of the unexpected bonus to get on to their objective. Their pioneers, working under small arms fire, lifted some fifty Teller mines, got the tanks through and the Battalion created a salient some 1,000 yards deep in the closely wooded country. There they would remain until the following day.

Sydney Jary now found his time with the Anti-Tank Platoon of 4 Som LI abruptly ended. He was transferred to D Company and 'quickly sucked into the real infantry battle' as commander of 18 Platoon. His predecessor was a casualty of the fighting at Briquessard as had been the company commander, who lost a foot from a *schuh* mine. His new platoon was down to seventeen all ranks and twelve of those were recent reinforcements: 'Hill 112 and Briquessard had claimed the rest.' (The war establishment of an infantry platoon was thirty-six men.)

To the right of the Som LI heavy shelling and machine-gun fire soon halted the left-hand company of 5 Dorset. Progress was better in the battalion centre, but on the right a dense minefield was encountered only three hundred yards from the start line. Tanks of A Squadron Sherwood Rangers moving with the battalion found the combination of hedges, ditches and mines made the going very slow. For the first time since the regiment had landed, one of their tanks was attacked by infantry firing German 'bazookas' (*Panzerfaust*). 'The first shells missed our tanks and one bazooka was promptly spotted and the crew liquidated.' The Regimental War Diary continued:

Infantry waiting for the track to be cleared of mines in the Normandy bocage.

Dorset Regiment.

After a lengthy interval of Red Indian stalking the troop located a second Bazooka which was captured with the crew. This troop had a busy day. The troop leader, Lt Render, himself dismounted and rendered harmless mines which had been hastily strewn on the surface by the retreating enemy. He also surprised a whole platoon of enemy walking in an exposed position on a small open field – unusual conduct for German Infantry. Fifteen of the enemy were killed and the remainder made prisoner.

The close country meant that further essential mine-clearance would have to wait for darkness. Later in the evening the Hampshire were therefore moved round the right flank of the Dorsets towards the ridge on which the village of Cahagnes stands. The battalion advanced astride the road leading to the village, but was soon seriously held up on the slopes of the ridge. A Company encountered minefields on the left and D Company met strong enemy opposition from the orchards on the right. However, the determined attack found all four companies in position three-quarters of the way up the slope by midnight. Several German counter-attacks were repulsed including a final attempt at daybreak next morning (31 July). That fierce attack, supported by intense mortar fire, was beaten off with heavy German losses.

Meanwhile an attack by 4 Dorset, with C Squadron Sherwood Rangers, on their left had opened the way for 7 Hampshire to advance on Cahagnes itself. They did not encounter much opposition but found the village badly damaged and fires still burning from the attacks by the RAF. Their supporting squadron from the Sherwood Rangers took several hours to negotiate the difficult approaches and found that even the Honey tanks of the regiment's Reconnaissance Troop were thwarted by the narrow, sunken tracks – not to mention the mines which had been laid on them. The Hampshires took up positions round the southern end of the village.

214 Brigade

214 Brigade, with 4/7 Dragoon Guards, 12 KRRC and three anti-tank batteries, could now advance from their waiting area east of Caumont-l'Éventé and the preliminary bombardment began. The left flank was open as 50th Division had not yet been able to secure Amayé- sur-Seulles and that was given particular attention by both the divisional artillery and the machine guns of 8 Middlesex, including laying a smoke screen. That and the cloud of dust raised by the dense traffic now covered the area in a thick cloud. Through it 1 Worcesters, leading the brigade, rode on the tanks of B Squadron 4/7 Dragoon Guards towards Caumont-l'Éventé and Cahagnes. After a minor action with some German infantry still holding out in front of Cahagnes, they were through the ruins of the village and a quarter of a mile further on when the leading company encountered an enemy company in some farm buildings. They were quickly engaged, but if the follow-up battalion, 7 Som LI, was not to be held up,

A British PIAT team.

time was of the essence. Another company of Worcestershires therefore by-passed the opposition and kept on to the objective a mile or so south of Cahagnes. By nightfall the battalion had consolidated and pushed out patrols who found the enemy in strength on the left flank. (Later that night 12 KRRC had a hard time guarding this flank.)

7 Som LI came forward in moonlight on the tanks of A Squadron, 4/7 Dragoon Guards. In Cahagnes they dismounted and, moving on foot through the Worcesters, advanced towards St Pierre-du-Fresne, two miles away. While they were searching buildings and orchards along the way, a German half-track arrived amongst them, and was quickly despatched by a PIAT bomb. When they reached the small village and consolidated amongst the solid farm buildings, they could hear sounds of enemy tank movement .

7th Armoured Division
    With the capture of Cahagnes, XXX Corps line was

sufficiently advanced for 7th Armoured Division to be brought forward to a concentration area about five miles north-east of Caumont.

St Germain d'Ectot, Launay and Amayé-sur-Seulles

Six weeks earlier, in mid June, XXX Corps had made a bold drive on Villers-Bocage in Operation PERCH. 7th Armoured Division, followed up by 50th Division, had driven through a gap in the German defences east of Tilly-sur-Seulles and enveloped the Panzer *Lehr* Division's left flank. 7th Armoured drove into Villers-Bocage to the elation of the inhabitants and it was in British hands for some hours. But the division was dangerously strung out and the imminent threat of strong German counter-attacks meant that the town had to be abandoned. The two divisions were now fighting over the same ground again, against greatly strengthened positions.

50th Division

For BLUECOAT, 50th Division was on the eastern flank of XXX Corps, with 56 Independent Infantry Brigade under command. The initial task for that brigade and 231 Brigade was to secure the Amayé-sur-Seulles feature, to the east of the Seulles stream. That was to be the preliminary to advancing, first on Villers-Bocage, then on Condé-sur-Noireau.

231 Brigade

At 0600 hrs on 30 July, 231 Brigade attacked from the area of la Croix des Landes and le Lion Vert with two battalions up – 1 Hampshire and 1 Dorset. Each had two troops from C Squadron 13/18 Hussars in support. Their first objective was the high ground north of St Germain d'Ectot. Initially the advance through the close country went well and leading companies were nearing the objective when enemy machine guns opened up at close range. After they had been silenced, the leading troops came under heavy artillery and mortar fire; they were now in direct view of German observers on the next range of hills. The thickly wooded area had to be cleared by tanks shooting up the infantry as they combed out small pockets of enemy. The advance was slow, but the Hampshires pushed on and captured the sunken road leading to Lictot from Ectot. The Dorsets on the left, held up by even thicker wooded country, eventually gained the same line as the Hampshires. They dug themselves in and later in the day the follow up companies could advance through them to the next brigade objective. They too met violent opposition, but the supporting tanks of C Squadron ('who fought with great dash and daring') helped them to secure the position by the end of the day.

At 0700 hrs on the 31st the brigade was on the move again through thick morning mist, this time with the Devons on the left. The Devons' objectives were Lictot and the high ground due west. The pace was slow because of the mist, but the opposition light. Two troops of AVREs, with the two troops from C Squadron, helped clear the enemy from Lictot so that the infantry could go straight through the village and consolidate to the east and south-east. It was Minden Day and, moving forward on the right, the Hampshires wore red roses in their helmets, picked from the wall of a ruined building. Their objective was the high ground at Launay; the enemy had held this strongly, but it was secured with but little opposition and fighting patrols sent down the Anctoville-Feuguerolles-sur-Seulles road came across no enemy. They had withdrawn farther south, but still continued very consistent shelling and mortaring.

56 Brigade

Attacking to the right of 231 Brigade was 56 Independent Brigade also with two battalions up and supported by A Squadron 13/18 Hussars. On the right 2 Gloucesters' initial objective was the high ground to the west of St Germain d'Ectot, with H Hour of 0630 hrs. By mid-day the battalion and a troop from A Squadron had made good progress and were on their objective, taking some fifty prisoners and about half a dozen Spandau machine guns. On the left, 2 South Wales Borderers were to have crossed the start line (the Caumont-Crauville road) an hour later than the Gloucesters, aiming at St Germain-d'Ectot itself. But they were held up by the late arrival of a troop of Crocodile flame-throwing tanks, which had broken down. It was some three and half hours before the battalion group could get across the start line. Flail tanks cleared lanes in a minefield for the accompanying troop from A Squadron who were providing 'suppressive fire', but by mid-day the South Wales Borderers had not been able to advance more than a third of the distance to their objective, during which they suffered casualties from severe enemy mortaring. However they had captured about forty prisoners and five or six machine guns. Meanwhile 2 Essex had passed through 2 Gloucesters, aiming at the Launay ridge, but they too were unable to get forward. During the afternoon an A Squadron troop leader and his troop sergeant had made a reconnaissance on foot with a platoon commander of the Essex, to try to find a way forward:

> *On their way back to their tanks they saw a badly wounded German soldier in a hedge and they went to investigate the condition of this man. Whilst bending over the man Lieutenant Spencer was hit in the thigh by a Spandau which opened up upon them.*

A further attempt with an additional troop and artillery support

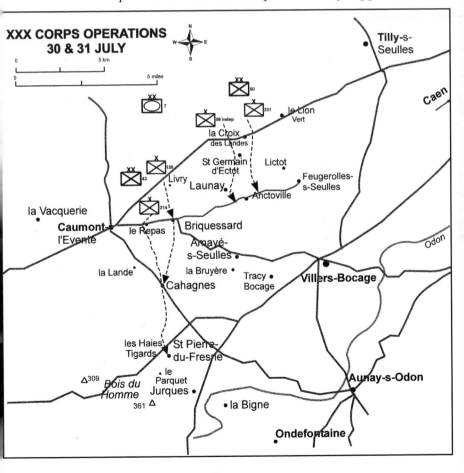

was also unsuccessful and the battalion suffered a number of casualties from enemy mortars. Derrick Wormald, commanding A Squadron 13th/18th, was left with the impression that the day's operations 'had lacked artillery support and that they had not been co-ordinated. My troops had been used in 'penny-packets' and the squadron had not been able to exert much influence on the proceedings.' But Pat Hennessey's crew had some light relief during the slow advance:

> *'...there suddenly emerged from the edge of the wood a very fat, middle-aged German Feldwebel, riding a horse. He took one look at us; his face became a study of shock and horror. He turned his horse and galloped back into the wood. Harry Bone shouted: "Shoot him, Shoot him!" but the incident was so hilarious that we did not have the heart to shoot. In the event, he later ran into a platoon of our infantry who took him prisoner.*

On 31 August, 2 SWB made a renewed attack on St Germain d'Ectot. A troop from A Squadron covered the clearance of mines by a section of flail tanks and the troop of tanks and one of Crocodiles then led the infantry forward. That was successful and the Brigade Commander wanted 2 Essex with A Squadron to tackle the Launay feature that evening. Ahead of the brigade was a formidable ditch; the country on the left was very enclosed and on the right there were fields and orchards. It was suspected that the enemy had laid mines south of St Germain-d'Ectot (beyond the planned start line). A fire plan was agreed involving three field regiments and two medium regiments – after Derrick Wormald had expressed concern that the proposed amount of artillery support would again be inadequate.

> *The fire plan was that a barrage should open at H Hour and move forward at 100 yards every five minutes down to the ditch where it would pause for ten minutes before proceeding up to the ridge and the village of Launay at 100 yards every six minutes. Smoke was to be mixed with the HE and also to be fired on the Right Flank of the attack throughout the   programme.*

The barrage opened at 2000 hrs and, as it moved forward, flail tanks under command of A Squadron created lanes, as a precaution against the probable mine field. All four troops of the squadron followed them through the lanes, keeping as close to the barrage as possible and engaging possible enemy positions as soon as the barrage had lifted from them. The two leading companies of 2 Essex followed the tanks. On reaching the ditch

Churchill flame-throwing tank 'Crocodile' in action.

there was a pause; but the obstacle was negotiated and the advance was continued. A sunken road then held up the tanks as they approached the village (on the right flank) but the infantry were close to the village and entered it without opposition as dusk fell.

The Commanding Officer and Adjutant of the 13th/18th had set off that evening to HQ 50th Division:

'...to get the news and go on and watch "A" Squadron battle who are to go across a stream about 600 yards in front of their line and establish themselves the other side. The news at Division is good – the Yanks are going Great Guns and are in and beyond Avranches which is terrific news. Went on to 'A' Squadron. Found them eventually with the attack in full swing and Peter Lyon behind a farm-full of dead cows and very smelly! Our barrage was going over our heads and the heavy machine guns were firing away, the infantry and tanks were going on

45

well about two fields ahead. The Colonel and I then went up to watch from the forward slope. Saw the tanks and infantry were leapfrogging forwards, shooting like mad. The place was littered with mines and booby traps, so couldn't go much further forward. In any case it would have been very unwise! On the way back we came under fire from our own machine guns while sitting on the outside of our scout car, which was fairly alarming.

As infantry occupied the village in front of them A Squadron rallied that night by troops rather than withdraw to a squadron harbour. The Squadron Leader leaguered with 2 Troop and during the night his crew stood-to when the man on watch heard a creaking noise approaching:

The main armament was on low depression, manned and ready to fire. Out of the darkness appeared the Troop Sergeant (Charlie Rattle – who had been the assistant Squadron Clerk as an unpaid lance corporal in 1936 or 37) wheeling a barrel of what turned out to be 'Eau de Vie de Mar' (local Brandy) on a farm barrow of which the wheel was in need of lubrication.

Chapter Three

30 and 31 July – VIII Corps

Progress on the 8 Corps flank proved easier than on 30 Corps front. The former advanced astride the Caumont-Bény Bocage road; La Fouquerie and Les Loges were soon reached.

NORMANDY TO THE BALTIC

On 30 July VIII Corps was to attack an hour later than XXX Corps. With 15th Scottish Division on the left and 11th Armoured on the right, they were to establish themselves in the area of St Martin-des-Besaces and, while protecting the right flank of XXX Corps, exploit round the Forêt l'Éveque to Point Aunay. If the situation permitted, 11th Armoured was to push on to the south and west irrespective of the progress of 15th Division.

Quarry Hill
15th Division and 6 Guards Tank Brigade

15th Division was the right-hand of the three infantry divisions in the centre of the BLUECOAT offensive. (On their left was 43rd Division, attacking in the centre.) The division's first objective on 30 July was to establish itself on Point 309 (Quarry Hill), a dominating feature west of the Bois du Homme [shown as Bois de Brimbois on some maps]. Under command of the division was 6 Guards Tank Brigade as well as one squadron from the Household Cavalry Regiment and one from the Lothian and Border Horse. The start line, laid down at Army level, ran one and half to two miles south of, and roughly parallel to, the ridge on which Caumont- l'Éventé stands. It was not clearly defined, having probably been set in a hurry to coincide with the safety line for the first bomber attack - itself an arbitrary line on the map. The enemy not only held this start line, but in the valley between it and Caumont he had two strong points at Sept-Vents and Bois Mondant (Lutaine Wood).

227 Brigade with the Guards Tank Brigade were therefore, first, to take those strong points, second, to advance south to take la Fouquerie, les Loges and Point 226, overlooking the northern end of Bois du Homme. 46 Brigade would then

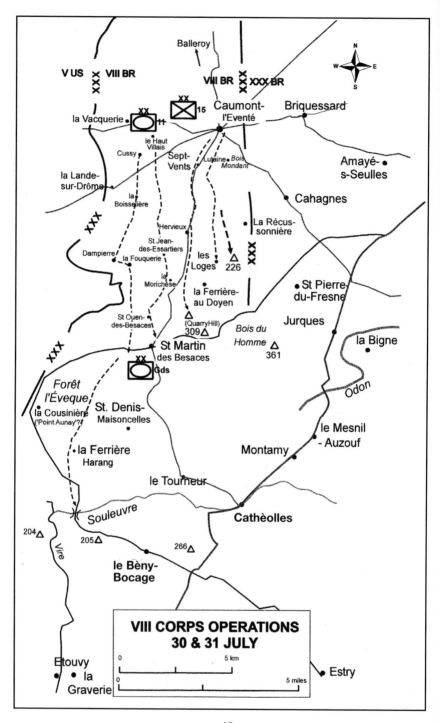

VIII CORPS OPERATIONS
30 & 31 JULY

advance on and secure Quarry Hill.

227 Brigade

During the previous night the leading troops formed up north of the start line: the main east and west road along the ridge and through Caumont-l'Éventé. An overcast dawn revealed on the reverse slopes of the ridge 'a milling crowd of tanks, carriers, half-tracks, Crocodiles, Flails, Infantry, all struggling to sort themselves out'. At 0655 hrs the Cameronians and the Gordons, each supported by tanks of 4 Grenadier Guards moved off down the valley. The other two battalions of 227 Brigade and their supporting arms followed. While they formed up (in full view) on the forward slopes, waiting for their start line to be secured for them, they saw 'a heartening sight':

Cameronians

Gordons

> *The air was filled with a great fleet of heavy and medium bombers – over 1,300 of them. They came, those Lancasters, Halifaxes, Mitchells; they dropped their bombs; in twos and threes they flew homeward only some two hundred feet above Caumont ridge.* (History of 15th Scottish Division)

After a morning's stiff fighting, the Gordons on the left had cleared the wood at Lutaine and dug in around it. On the right the Cameronians attacked astride a narrow, sunken lane leading to Sept-Vents, which was to be the Corps' axis. The supporting tanks, unable to deploy because of the steep banks, tried to get forward along the lane, but it was 'very thoroughly mined' and a Churchill minus its tracks soon blocked it. Delayed action mines frustrated the opening up of the lane and clearing Sept-Vents itself was a slow process. However, by 1500 hrs the axis was open.

The follow up brigades of 15th Division had not been able to wait; they had to cross the Army start line at 0955 hrs in order to conform to the planned artillery barrage. But the forward companies of the HLI and the Argylls were soon under mortar and machine-gun fire as they went down into the valley. Their half-tracks and carriers could not get across the dense country and all the lanes were blocked by a variety of other vehicles. The Argylls tried to move round to the west of Lutaine Wood, only to run into an anti-personnel minefield. The German defences ran in depth as far as the Army start line and there was no question of the attacking infantry battalions reaching it in time. However, their supporting tanks from 4 Coldstream and 3 Scots Guards, did force their way through more or less on time, 'doing considerable execution with their Besas and high-explosive against machine-gun posts and strong-points on the way'.

At about 0930 hrs they pushed on from the start line, without the infantry, in order to benefit from the artillery barrage. The difficult country slowed them down, but by 1130 hrs the Coldstream had reached Hervieux and the Scots Guards were in la Récussonnière. The HLI caught up with the Coldstream in Hervieux and they went on together to take the high ground, eight hundred yards farther south, by about 1500 hrs.

Following up the Scots Guards, the Argylls did not reach the start line until about 1300 hrs and had to halt while a revised fire plan was laid on. The forward squadrons of the Scots Guards had gone on alone and by 1430 hrs had occupied Hill 226, on the left of their objective. Not long afterwards the leading company of the Argylls reached les Loges and two more of their companies had arrived on Hill 226 by 1530 hrs. But the Argylls were without transport and anti-tank guns and 3 Scots Guards therefore remained with them, hull-down on the crest, with the infantry on the reverse slope.

By this time 43rd Division should have been closing on the Bois du Homme, but they were still fighting for the crossings at Briquessard. The left flank of 15th Division was wide open and 44 Brigade was ordered to cover it.

46 Brigade

46 Brigade had moved up in order to pass through 227 Brigade in the final phase, but the Glasgow Highlanders and the Seaforth soon ran into the same sort of trouble with mines and transport blocks as had the HLI and the Argylls. They reached the forward assembly area by about 1500 hrs only by striking across country. An hour later two waves of Marauder medium bombers passed overhead, on their way to bomb Quarry Hill. At that stage 46 Brigade and their armour should have been able to assault the hill. However, the division was now getting too strung out so that advance was cancelled and 4 Coldstream Guards were sent forward on their own. They found la

Morichèse occupied by the Germans and by-passed it, heading across country to establish themselves above the quarry – of Quarry Hill – having negotiated bogs and springs en route, but without meeting any opposition. They could now look down into Bois du Homme to the east and across to Hill 361 where, if all had gone well, 43rd Division would now have been arriving. Instead they were alone, nearly six miles deep in enemy lines.

Glasgow Highlanders

It was clearly necessary to get infantry to Quarry Hill as soon as possible and 4 Grenadiers were sent to pick up the Glasgow Highlanders north of Hervieux crossroads and lift them forward so that they could take over from the Coldstream before dark. That was easier said than done. The tanks found a traffic jam in Hervieux; the main axis was crowded with a variety of vehicles, many of them having strayed from 11th Armoured Division further west. They then fell foul, not only of a well-concealed 88mm

Seaforth Highlanders

in la Morichèse, but of cannon-fire from some ME 109's who demonstrated that Allied air supremacy was not total. Dusk was approaching and it became obvious that the Glasgow Highlanders would do better on foot. Even so it was not until 0230 hrs next day that the last of the Glasgow Highlanders' rifle companies reached Quarry Hill and could take over its defence. With them were the battalion anti-tank guns, many of which had had to be manhandled; their carriers found the rough ground almost impassable. The Seaforth were also on their way up to the hill and, after a very difficult advance through enemy country, they arrived before dawn and linked up with the Glasgow Highlanders.

227 Brigade

The previous evening, at 1800 hrs, enemy mortars had put down 'a very heavy stonk' on the Argylls and Scots Guards, holding Hill 226. That was followed immediately by rapid fire from a high-velocity gun to the left rear whose first three shots knocked out the Scots Guards troop watching that flank. They came from two *Jagd* Panthers which, in a brilliant piece of field

A column of Sherman tanks advancing south of Caumont on 31 July.

craft, emerged from a wood and, covered by a third, climbed deliberately up the hill and through the position. They destroyed eight more Churchills at point-blank range before making their way over the crest in front. Fortunately they had no infantry with them and Hill 226 remained secure.

44 Brigade

At dawn the Germans were still in the Bois du Homme and on the high ground to the north and north-west of it. The troops on Quarry Hill had enemy on three sides with German SP guns in la Ferrière as well as strong elements in St Martin and along the railway line. The 31st would be spent largely in beating off determined counter-attacks, but the division consolidated the ground they had won and, by evening, had reached the crest of the ridge. In the afternoon 44 Brigade, with their supporting tanks, had been ordered to take the high ground north-west of Bois du Homme and link up with 46 Brigade on Quarry Hill and the Argylls in les Loges. In the process they had to run the gauntlet, not only of several attacks by RAF Typhoons, but also of shelling by XXX Corps' artillery – by this time 43rd Division was fighting in the eastern edges of the Bois du Homme round St Pierre-du-Fresne and Jurques.

St. Martin-des-Besaces
11th Armoured Division

During the night of 28-29 July, 11th Armoured Division formed up between Balleroy and Caumont-l'Éventé. It was operating with four battle groups: 23 Hussars with 3 Monmouthshire, 2 Fife and Forfarshire Yeomanry with 4 King's Shropshire Light Infantry, 3 Royal Tank Regiment with 1 Herefordshire; and 2 Northamptonshire Yeomanry with 8 Rifle Brigade. They were to protect the right flank of 15th Division and maintain contact with the American 5th Infantry Division's on their own right. 2 Household Cavalry armoured cars led 11th Armoured, followed by the battle groups in two columns advancing across a two-mile front. The left-hand column was directed from la Vallée (south-west of Caumont) bypassing Sept-Vents and keeping east of Dampierre. On the right the attack was via Cussy, la Boisselière and Dampierre. The two columns were to converge on St Martin-des-Besaces.

Before they could cross their start lines both 3 Monmouthshire and 1 Herefords suffered heavy casualties. As was happening elsewhere across the BLUECOAT front these came from mines laid by both friend and foe as well as from heavy German mortar and shell fire The Herefords secured a line of lightly held enemy posts, along a low ridge covered with orchards, only to find themselves under directly observed, accurate fire on ground where digging in was frustrated by rocky ground covered with only a thin layer of soil. There they had to wait until midday before the bombing programme, delayed by fog, could begin. Then they could advance, only to find the area strewn with *schuh* mines and meeting resistance from enemy machine guns in the hedges and woods round their objective – Cussy. However, with first class support from their own artillery Cussy was taken by 1800. 4 KSLI then passed through them with 2 Fife and Forfar.

3 Mons and the 23 Hussars were mortared and shelled heavily, but eventually reached Sept-Vents and cleared it with

the assistance of flail tanks at about 1430. When they moved along the main street: 'There was no living soul to be seen, just a few dead bodies.' 2 Fife and Forfarshire lost several tanks from mines at the start line but they and 4 KSLI found that the enemy they encountered – from 326th Infantry Division – were disorganised and scared; a high proportion were non-German. During the battlegroup's advance from Dampierre to la Fouquerie, they took 150 prisoners. The Fife and Forfars had been told to move on at speed:

It was a case of motoring flat out, 35 mph on the straight, for the faster you went the harder you were to hit. There were Germans all over the place, running and scampering. We fired wildly at them, overtook them and left them far behind. There were targets at every turn of the road. It was exhilarating.

La Boisselière was captured by 2nd Fife and Forfarshire and 4 KSLI while 3 Mons and 23 Hussars were fighting their way south to St Jean-des-Essartiers; they then took the hamlet of St Ouen-des-Besaces.

During the night H Company of 8 RB pushed on again to reach the Caumont – St Martin road, and by early morning was established north and east of St Martin-des-Besaces.

General 'Pip' Roberts, the Divisional Commander, later wrote – somewhat deprecatingly – that at dusk, 'Progress was slow but it had been made'.

After a very tiring approach march, and little sleep, and then a hard day's fighting there was a natural tendency to call it a day as soon as the sun went down but firm orders came from the Corps Commander that we could not relax. The main village in front of us was St Martin-des-Besaces; it was an important cross-roads; one main road ran east-west and the other north-south. We could hold it in front and attack from the west...

Before dawn on the 31st, 4 KSLI reached the outskirts of St Martin-des-Besaces, having set off at 0400 hrs and marched some three miles in single file on a very dark night along a woodland trail – unwatched by the enemy. At 0930 hrs with a squadron of 2 Fife & Forfar, they launched their attack on the town, followed up by 8 Rifle Brigade. Meanwhile 2 Household Cavalry were exploring the neighbouring roads and tracks and, in a great stroke of luck, a half-troop made its way unchallenged through the Forêt l'Évêque. They had used a track which turned out to have been a boundary between German divisions, each of

German Panther tank emerging from camouflage.

which thought of it as the other's responsibility. They found a
bridge intact across the River Souleuvre, five miles south and
called for reinforcements. This was wonderful news and 2
Northants Yeomanry and 4 KSLI, were ordered forward
immediately. They reached the bridge four hours after it had
been by taken by the Household Cavalry, much to the latter's
relief.

The RAF had reported that a German mechanised column
(from 21st Panzer Division) had crossed the Orne and was
heading for le Bény-Bocage; it approached from the east as the

Northants Yeomanry with 4 KSLI on their tanks came south. The Germans were put to flight after a short action. The next problem was created by troops of V US Corps 'whose map reading persuaded them that their boundary was 2 miles further west than originally agreed.' Friend and foe alike were having problems with their boundaries. VIII Corps Commander now instructed 11th Armoured Division:

> '...to capture the high ground round Point Aunay tonight so that the advance to Étouvy can proceed rapidly tomorrow. You should occupy tonight Point 204, Point 205 and the high ground east of le Bény-Bocage about Point 266. 2 Household Cavalry will tonight patrol south with utmost vigour in direction Vire.

Guards Armoured Division

In the late afternoon, Guards Armoured had advanced along the main road from Caumont to Vire, with 5 Guards Brigade in the lead. They were to occupy as much as possible of the ridge beyond St Martin before dusk, with a view to crossing the Souleuvre next day. It was soon all too obvious that the ridge was in German hands. The leading squadron rushed up the slope, but the following infantry were met by heavy machine-gun fire as dusk fell and a halt was called with a view to making an attack early next day.

* * * *

By dusk of 30 July 4th US Armoured Division had reached Avranches. The following day von Kluge told General Jodl, the Chief of Operations Staff at OKW:

> As a result of the break-through of the enemy armoured spearheads, the whole western front has been ripped open. ...The left flank has collapsed.

Chapter Four

1 & 2 August: XXX Corps

30 Corps brought 7 Armoured Division in on the left flank and directed it on Aunay-sur-Odon, while 50 Division made further progress towards Villers Bocage. 43 Division continued its advance during the night with the object of securing Ondefontaine, and was to be followed up by 7 Armoured Division at first light in the morning. On 2 August, 43 Division, having made good progress during the night, moved forward towards Aunay while 50 Division secured Amayé and continued the advance up the Seulles valley.

NORMANDY TO THE BALTIC

43rd Division
St Pierre-du-Fresne and Bois du Homme
214 Brigade

In St Pierre-du-Fresne 7 Som LI had heard tank movement during the night of 31 July/1 August. Sure enough, a patrol from A Company, which went out soon after dawn, reported a Tiger tank about 300 yards away. The company commander, Major J. K. Whitehead, decided to stalk it through the morning mist, only to find, as visibility improved, that several hundred German infantry were advancing towards his position from the opposite slope. His call for support brought down heavy fire from the whole of 43rd Division's artillery, but two large self-propelled guns (*Jagd* Panthers) – with infantry closely supporting them – had reached the forward platoons via a

German *Jagd* Panther self-propelled gun.

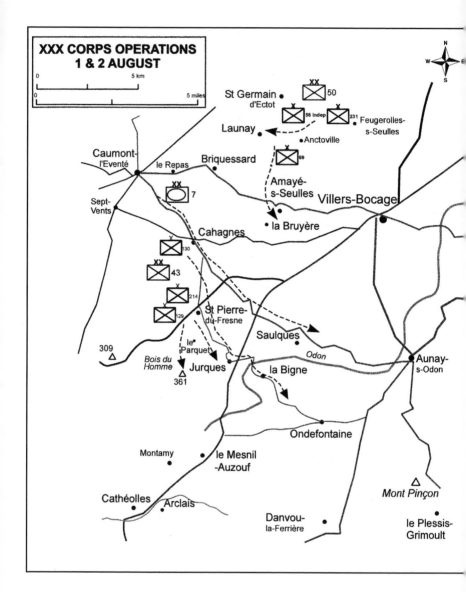

**XXX CORPS OPERATIONS
1 & 2 AUGUST**

sunken road. Several accounts refer to 'Ferdinand' self-propelled guns, but there is no record of that model appearing in the West; the War Diary of the Sherwood Rangers terms the SPs encountered: 'Jaguars' and '*Jagdpanthers*' attacked 15th Division the same day. There was fierce fighting with the enemy infantry during which the SPs were firing constantly until one withdrew, blinded by phosphorous grenades hitting its turret and the other was abandoned by its crew. Still in gear it continued to grind slowly forward. That was the end of the battle. During it A Company had exhausted its stock of grenades and smoke bombs, but had killed over twenty Germans and taken forty more prisoners. Their own losses were four killed and seven wounded.

Another company of 7 Som LI, at the left rear of the battalion, had been being attacked at the same time and that assault had also been beaten off. Amongst the prisoners were men of 21st Panzer Division, the first of the enemy's armoured divisions to appear on the scene. Later in the morning, what was left of a German regiment of three battalions – the commander, his adjutant and fifty-eight other ranks – surrendered to 1 Worcestershire.

The division had penetrated the German defence line and the area around and behind 214 Brigade had not been cleared of the enemy. A sizeable enemy position south of Cahagnes was not finally cleared up until systematically attacked by the DCLI, while four miles north-east, the enemy still held out Amayé-sur-Seulles. Two more panzer divisions, 9th and 10th SS, were now arriving and stiffer resistance could be expected.

129 Brigade

129 Brigade now advanced to Bois du Homme. As soon as 7 Som LI had beaten off the counter-attack on St Pierre-du-Fresne, 5 Wiltshire headed due south towards Point 361 [358] on the thickly wooded hill. After various encounters with the enemy, including one with a German Red Cross vehicle stuffed with bread and loot and another with a scout car of 9th SS Panzer Division, the battalion deployed to assault the hill, making their way up through the trees along a the variety of tracks. As the leading companies dug in on the top three *Jagdpanther* self-propelled guns and an armoured car plunged in amongst them. One became bogged and was quickly dealt with but the other two forged through one of the company positions, shooting as they went. When the first ditched that was soon put out of action the other turned back and ran over some men of A Company before being knocked out by a British SP gun, which had just appeared below the ridge.

4 Wiltshire moved up on the right flank, taking some

prisoners, and began a nightlong preparation against further counter-attacks. Getting the anti-tank guns up the 200-foot slope required forty men to manhandle each gun. During the night there was a torrential storm; the tracks up the hill became almost impassable and slit trenches filled with water.

A Squadron, Sherwood Rangers supported 5 Wiltshire in a thrust to Point 361, south of Bois du Homme and advanced steadily against opposition which was not strong, but did include a *Jagd* Panther self-propelled gun and three Tiger tanks. The *Jagd* and one Tiger were destroyed and the other two Tigers became bogged and could be captured.

Divisional plans had been for Bois du Homme to be secure and le Mesnil Auzouf captured before continuing to Ondefontaine. However, with 129 Brigade fully committed on the slopes of Bois du Homme, an immediate advance on Ondefontaine was required if 43rd Division were to make more rapid progress.

Knocked out German Tiger tank at the side of the road.

Jurques and la Bigne

130 Brigade was therefore given the task of taking Jurques, la Bigne and Ondefontaine and 4 Dorset were to take the lead. With their supporting arms they formed up just before midnight of 1 August; B Squadron Sherwood Rangers in the van. They reached Jurques without opposition, but between there and la Bigne were halted by mines and suffered casualties from mortar and small arms fire. Two of the Sherwood Rangers' tanks were destroyed and it was some hours before la Bigne could be occupied. The advance resumed only to be halted a short distance south of the village. Under the cover of darkness German aircraft ventured a sortie and parachute flares, followed up by anti-personnel bombs, lit the area. But these dropped well clear of the 4 Dorset group, which set off again at 0115 on 2 August. Platoons were lifted on tanks and the battalion carrier platoon led the column through the pitch dark. They saw a light flicker as they approached Cahagnes and at the crossroads found one of the divisional military police; he thought he was in Caumont.

Soon after 0900 hrs the leading company encountered mines on the heavily cratered road half a mile short of Jurques and met the first opposition from a small number of Germans holding out in the battered village. In the hilly and close country ahead there was plenty of scope for the enemy to impose delay and they soon engaged the Dorsets from the flanks bringing down massive fire from a variety of weapons, including self-propelled guns and machine guns. As A Company neared the top of the hill on the approaches to la Bigne they suffered severely from the very heavy fire. Nevertheless, the battalion pioneers and their accompanying engineers set about clearing the mines on the approaches and, once that was done, two more companies supported by tanks renewed the assault. The village was finally captured by 1600 hrs.

The battalion's patrols found more enemy, in strength, in the woods beyond la Bigne and in Ondefontaine. 5 Dorset were ordered to take on the advance the following morning. Behind them in Jurques, 7 Hampshire were being shelled heavily and were unsuccessful in their efforts during that day and the following night to advance south, despite RAF Typhoons tackling Tiger tanks on the dominating high ground ahead of them. 'The fact had to be faced that the Division was once more up against determined and well-organized opposition on ground which gave every advantage to the enemy.'

Launay, Amayé-sur-Seulles, la Bruyère

50th Division

231Brigade and 56 Independent Brigade

56 and 231 Brigades had pressed forward to the high ground between Anctoville and Feuguerolles-sur-Seulles and were firmly entrenched there by 1 August. Both brigades resumed the advance at 0700 hrs, through a heavy morning mist, in order to occupy the high feature at Launay, which the enemy had been holding strongly. The poor visibility made it impracticable for the assaulting battalions to be accompanied by tanks. However, most of the Germans had now withdrawn and the leading

A Sherman covers the advance of a British column during Operation BLUECOAT.

companies reached the objective against little opposition, although they still came under persistent shelling and mortaring.

69 Brigade

The 13/18 Hussars, still with 50th Division, were told that they were to attack Amayé-sur-Seulles and la Bruyère next morning with 69 Brigade:

> '... the Colonel and I went off to do our evening round, and after going to 8 Brigade and on to look for 'A' met Gen. Graham, 50 Division, on the road ... After, we had a drink with a French farmer in his completely ruined farm. There was hardly a building left standing and most of his cattle were dead – very dead, and lying about the farmyard. The stench was appalling. He was delighted to see us and volubly discussed things, most of which I couldn't understand. The General had said we were to go and discuss the attack with Brigadier 69 and off we went. The roads were beyond belief – absolutely solid with 7th Armoured and 69 Brigade pushing on to exploit the breakthrough. It was an incredible sight – the dust was appalling and a dozen Boche aircraft could have caused absolute havoc. ...'

The 69 Brigade plan was for 7 Green Howards, supported by A Squadron 13/18 Hussars, to advance on the left to tackle Amayé village and the high ground round it while 5 East Yorks to the right, supported by B Squadron, advanced on la Bruyère. H Hour was to be 1600 hrs on 2 August. That morning, Julius Neave went with his Commanding Officer and the two squadron leaders to Headquarters 69 Brigade, to lay on the attack.

> ... By this time it was uncertain if it would be required as they reckoned the Boche were pulling out. However, old Graham turned up later to say it was now 'on' and instead of at 1600 hrs as we had hoped it was now to be at 1300 hrs! So panic moves and recces started and luckily we all got there on time, which was no mean effort. Recces in this area (SE of Caumont-Cahagnes-Briquessard etc.) are no fun, it is completely devastated and very smelly – in one ruined village where there was apparently not a soul we found a very old man indeed still digging his garden. He gave us a broad grin as we went on.

Contact had first to be made with 214 Brigade of 43rd Division, a short distance westwards, who had come down the road from Briquessard, reaching a small ridge some 1,200 yards west of Amayé. The CO 7 Green Howards with Derrick Wormald, commanding A Squadron, visited them: 'The commander of these troops informed us that there were no enemy in or on our Objective area.' This drew from Derrick Wormald the sardonic comment:

This seemed to be an inexactitude, because at the time there was a considerable amount of unmistakeable Spandau fire being directed at, we thought, his forward elements. It was not, therefore, considered to be a suitable area in which to discus our plan for the advance/attack.

When they returned to HQ 69 Brigade at about 1200 hrs, they met Major General Thomas, GOC 43rd Division, 'who also told us that there were no enemy on the objective; but that it was possible that they would move their armour onto the high ground to oppose our advance, we should therefore capture it with all haste.' They also heard that H Hour had been brought forward to 1300. A Squadron were only just leaving their harbour area at Crauville, en route for an assembly area for a 1600 hrs attack. The second-in-command was told by wireless to bring them speedily to a forming-up point just short of the 214 Brigade outposts, on the road from Briquessard. The plan was for A Squadron to occupy the ridge to the north of Amayé as quickly as possible whilst the battalion would occupy the village. Time would not allow for CO 7 Green Howards to hold an O Group for company commanders to issue their orders and get the battalion to their start line by 1300 hrs. One company was therefore to be carried forward on a troop of tanks accompanied by the battalion carrier platoon, protecting the right flank. 'Company HQ was to be carried on the troop leader's tank and each other tank in the troop was to carry a platoon of about thirty men and their kit – quite a crush and a balancing act, especially when travelling across country.'

A Squadron reached their FUP just before 1300 hrs, and received their orders from Major Wormald on the move. Leaving behind the troop detailed to carry the Green Howards' company, they moved off. Two troops fanned out to the left of the road, one heading direct for the high ground while the other covered what was an open left flank. The third troop came up on their right to cover the orchards surrounding the village and soon reported that they were engaging with maximum firepower a sizeable number of enemy. The troop carrying the company of Green Howards was now approaching the village and they and the carrier platoon came under Spandau fire. The

Congestion among the hedgerows.

infantry hurriedly dismounted and a pre-arranged fire plan was requested.

When that ended and the troop engaging the orchards temporarily ceased firing over a hundred enemy came out from the orchards with their arms up and surrendered to the troop who simply waved them back along the road. 'They willingly complied with the signals given to them.' However, Spandau fire still held up the infantry until the fire plan was repeated when they could move forward with the right hand troop of tanks. The remainder of the squadron reached their objective unopposed and took up hull down positions. By 1800 hrs the Green Howards were in the orchards on the forward slopes of the village, having taken nearly sixty prisoners, but, after the village was captured Captain Lyon was killed by a sniper who shot him in the head whilst he was standing in his tank.

Lance Corporal Pat Hennessey was present when Captain Peter Lyon was killed:

We had halted in the area of a crossroads when the second-in-

Lance Corporal Pat Hennessy 13th/18th Hussars.

command of the Squadron, Captain Peter Lyon, called me over to his tank. I climbed up and spoke to him as we studied his map; I was standing on the side of his tank and he leaning out of the turret. I jumped down and was walking back to my own tank when I heard the unmistakeable sound of a burst of Schmeisser sub-machine gun fire. Captain Lyon lay slumped across the top of his turret, shot through the head by a sniper. I joined in the fusillade of fire we sent up into the trees from which the sniper had fired, and we had the satisfaction of getting him, but we were all terribly sad at losing Captain Lyon, who was a most efficient and very popular officer. For my part, I could not help reflecting that I had just had a very narrow escape.

Pat Hennessey's troop leader was Lieutenant Hugh Elliot, who had joined the 13th/18th as a replacement troop leader shortly after D Day:

... we came under fire which we repulsed with the excellent 0.300 Brownings of the Shermans. Sadly our 2IC, Captain Peter Lyon, was shot in the head by a sniper and another sniper punctured my tin hat,

Lieutenant Hugh Elliot 13th/18th Hussars.

grazing my skull, but nothing serious. Tank commanders, in close country, were very vulnerable to this form of attack, especially as, in the Sherman, the inadequate periscope necessitated a head and shoulders stance out of the turret, in order to see both friend and foe.

The 5 E Yorks group had encountered much more difficult country and it was 1900 hrs before they took la Bruyère – and a number of prisoners.

7th Armoured Division

During the thick morning mist of 1 August, 7th Armoured Division had moved forward from the Caumont area, aimed at Aunay-sur-Audon. They had to make their way between 43rd and 50th Division and, as Julius Neave had

Germans clearing a village in Normandy.

found, roads all round Caumont were heavily congested. (A Canadian officer offered his solution: 'What beats me, is why we don't bring over one London bobby to control the traffic, and we'd be out of here in no time'). They also found that 'the whole area was covered with mines and there were many enemy infantry posts who were determined to stay and fight'. The armoured cars of the 11 Hussars took three hours to cover twelve miles on the main road, and it was 2030 hrs before 1 RTR and a squadron of 8 Hussars were clear of 50th Division and had reached three miles south-east of Cahagnes, where mines and infantry put a stop to any further progress that day.

On 2 August the advance resumed at 0600 with the 8 Hussars and the Inniskillings on the left of 1 RTR. They met steady opposition throughout the day, but by evening C Squadron 1 RTR had taken the high ground north-west of Saulques; it had cost them six tanks and twenty-four casualties. 5 and 7 Queen's secured the areas gained during the day while 6 Queen's prepared a night attack onto the high ground further east. Aunay-sur-Odon was still in German hands, although the 8 Hussars were only three miles to the north-west.

Command Changes

By now, the lack of progress by XXX Corps, particularly by 7th Armoured Division, was considered unacceptable and Lieutenant General Bucknall, the Corps Commander, is said to have been told to 'get on or get out'. On 2 August he was replaced by Lieutenant General Horrocks, whose briefing by General Montgomery concluded:

The key tactical feature now in our advance is Mont Pinçon, which dominates the surrounding country and must be captured as soon as possible. It is on XXX Corps' front so that will be your first major problem.

Brigadier Verney from 6 Guards Tank Brigade replaced Major General Erskine as Commander 7th Armoured Division. The Commander 22 Armoured Brigade and the Commander Royal Artillery, together with more than a hundred other officers of the division, were also posted away. Not surprisingly this further disrupted the effective operation of 7th Armoured, not only during Operation BLUECOAT, but for some time to come. (It was said that they did not recover the greatness of their desert campaigns until the North German Plain was reached the following year.)

Chapter Five

1 & 2 August: VIII Corps

On 1 August 8 Corps cleared le Bény Bocage, and the Guards made for Estry; 15 Division, holding a firm base for the armour, repulsed counter-attacks delivered by the enemy from the south and south-east. ... On 2 August .... Opposition to 8 Corps was now becoming more stubborn; elements of 11 Armoured Division reached the northern outskirts of Vire and patrols crossed the Vire-Vassy road, but the enemy had not evacuated Vire and there were signs of his being reinforced in the area south of Mont Pinçon. The Air Force found good targets among tanks and vehicles moving west in the Condé area. In its advance on Estry, Guards Armoured Division met heavy opposition and was eventually held up. **Normandy to the Baltic**

British and American troops using the same roads during the advance in Normandy.

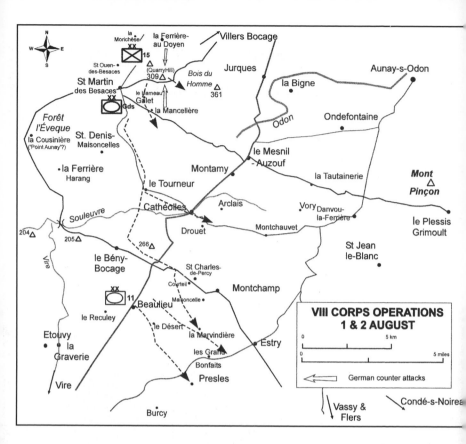

VIII Corps

Household Cavalry armoured cars had found Vire almost deserted on the night of 1/2 August, but the town was on the American side of the boundary between the two Armies and was one of General Bradley's objectives. VIII Corps was therefore told to make its main drive south-east towards Flèrs. By this time it was known that 9th SS, 10th SS and 21st Panzer Divisions had been hurriedly moved across from the east to oppose the BLUECOAT advance and 3rd Infantry Division reinforced VIII Corps.

Quarry Hill
15th Division

15th (Scottish) Division, providing a firm base for the two armoured divisions of VIII Corps, was having to hold on against renewed counter-attacks. On 31 July/1 August they had had a quiet night on Quarry Hill, but with daylight on 1 August came a heavy concentration of artillery and mortar fire and the enemy tried again and again to infiltrate the positions on the southern slopes. Infantry and tanks of 21st Panzer Division attacked both from the south and from la Ferrière, but were repeatedly dispersed by the British artillery. The final attack came at about 1600 hrs when a strong force of tanks and infantry appeared out of the Bois du Homme to the east as well as from the north-east. 'They were met by everything we had got – medium and field artillery, 4.2 and 3-

**15th (Scottish)
Division**

Following a failed attack a German prisoner is being searched.

inch mortars, medium machine-guns.' By 1800 the Germans were withdrawing, after losing six Tiger tanks as well as a number of prisoners.

The Cameronians in and around St Martin-des-Besaces were now ordered to clear Galet and la Mancellière. With support from the Coldstream and the Divisional Reconnaissance Regiment, that was achieved against only slight opposition during the afternoon. There were then reports that a large force of German armour was advancing into the gap from the Bois du Homme and, in late afternoon, the KOSB and the Grenadiers advanced up the spur of la Ferrière. (The KOSB was another 'Minden regiment' and they too were wearing roses in their helmets.) After a stiff fight in the wood they reached the road from St Martin-des-Besaces to Villers-Bocage and linked up at last with 43rd Division.

On 2 August, 227 Brigade, with 3 (Tank) Scots Guards took over Hill 238/244 from 5 Coldstream and 2 (Armoured) Irish Guards and Guards Armoured Division was able to continue its advance on Vassy with 15th Divisional Reconnaissance Regiment following up and watching the left flank. 9th and 10th SS Panzer Divisions were now arriving, but 15th Division held their firm base on Quarry Hill and Hill 238/244.

Le Tourneur, the Arclais and Drouet hills, St Charles-de-Percy
Guards Armoured Division

At dawn on 1 August, 5 Guards Brigade had resumed their attack on the ridge beyond St Martin-des-Besaces; 15th Division had identified the reconnaissance regiment of 21st Panzer Division the previous evening. It was soon clear that tanks and infantry from that division had been thrown in immediately on arrival across the VIII Corps' axis. Here, too, there was a morning of very heavy fighting before the Germans could be moved off the ridge. With their Panthers and Tigers, as well as the natural defences of the *bocage*, they took heavy toll of 5 Guards Brigade in the process. While the brigade consolidated the ground that had been won, 32 Guards Brigade came up to resume the advance. In a demonstration that the Germans still had observation over much of the area their Brigade O Group was shelled, causing many casualties. However, 3 Irish Guards, with a squadron of Coldstream tanks, were able quickly to drive the enemy off the end of the ridge above the le Tourneur valley.

Men of the Irish Guards and a Sherman belonging to the Coldstream Guards making their way along a road near St Martin des Besaces.

The King's Company of the Grenadiers and a troop of Irish Guards tanks then attempted to rush the bridge in le Toumeur, but there was only an hour of daylight left and the village had more Germans than they could deal with in the failing light. Two companies of the Irish Guards set off in the early hours and before daylight the battalion held le Tourneur. They then pushed down the Tourneur valley to where it meets the Souleuvre and crossed the bridge, to find that 11th Armoured Division had already occupied le Bény-Bocage and the crossroads at St Charles-de-Percy.

Grenadier Guards

From the Souleuvre valley the Cromwells of 2 Welsh Guards, their reconnaissance battalion, preceded Guards Armoured Division on 2 August in two thrusts. The Grenadier Group followed the valley heading for Montchauvet, across the hills west of Mont Pinçon, while the Coldstream-Irish Group went on, via St Charles-de-Percy, towards Montchamp and Estry. The Cathéolles bridge was crossed without incident early in the day, but on the

ColdstreamGuards

Scots Guards

Irish Guards

Welsh Guards

narrow, winding road beyond the Welsh Guards encountered sniping and mortaring and just before Montchauvet their leading tank was hit and set on fire. The road was completely blocked and diversion was not feasible; the route was handed over to the Grenadiers. Meanwhile another Welsh Guards squadron was checked at Courteil, just beyond St Charles-de-Percy, and the area seemed full of resolute Germans. However, the going here was easier and the squadron succeeded in making their way round and reached the high ground south of la Marvindière, only for their patrols to meet strong opposition between there and Estry.

In order to get on, the Grenadier group had to seize the spur on which Drouet stood; they also had to get the Germans off the Arclais hill on the north side of the valley. An attack on the Arclais hill failed; it was strongly held and too steep for supporting tanks. Drouet was occupied for a while, but an evening counter-attack with tanks forced a withdrawal from the village to a precarious position on the crest of the spur.

The Irish-Coldstream Group, forced to halt while the Grenadiers fought their way forward, were heavily shelled and mortared by the Germans on both the Drouet and Arclais hills. Eventually their tanks succeeded in forcing a way through and carried the Coldstream infantry through the defile to St Charles-de-Percy. Like the Welsh Guards they found all approaches to Courteil barred and they too went south across country and harboured just short of la Marvindière.

The Presles-Burcy ridge
11th Armoured Division

Meanwhile 11th Armoured Division had forged on and cut the Caen/Vire road beyond St Charles-de-Percy. Divisional HQ had reached le Reculey, 1½ miles south-west of le Bény-Bocage. Looking south from Bény-Bocage two ridges could be seen that obviously commanded the whole of the area between and the ground to either side. They run from north-east to south-west;

the first is about four miles from Bény-Bocage and the second, higher one, is a mile and a half further on.

'August 2nd was going to be an exciting day', wrote General Roberts. 'We were clearly going to be out on our own as on both flanks there appeared to be more opposition than in front of us, but on the right the Germans seemed to have reinforced Vire.' His main objective was to be the cutting of the main road from Vire to Vassy, east of Vire.

At the end of 2 August, after a day of hard fighting, the division had advanced seven miles and held a front of over three miles along the Presles-Burcy ridge. They had also cut the main road from Vire to Vassy in two places, but the cost had included thirty-one tanks and opposition was increasing. The Shermans of the 23 Hussars had taken particularly heavy punishment and, in one 'short, sharp engagement', their A Squadron lost five men killed and a dozen wounded in a few minutes. The Squadron Leader had been badly wounded and, at one stage, two troops were missing and it looked as though the

German Panther tank.

whole squadron was going to be destroyed.

Near St Charles-de-Percy the advance by another of the division's regimental groups, 4 KSLI and 3 RTR, had been slowed down by small groups of Germans disputing every piece of ground. The KSLI were able eventually to dig in for the night west of the small hamlet of les Grand Bonfait. (When the leading company commander, Major Thornbum, took a patrol towards the small hamlet he caught sight of three Panther tanks advancing in the dusk on the 3 RTR leaguer. Just in time he was able to warn them over a 38 set.)

The narrow roads on what was only a narrow corridor behind them meant that any replenishment for the division was going to be very limited. However, the Corps Commander, who was heavily shelled during a visit to Divisional HQ at le Reculey, agreed with General Roberts that the best course of action was to hold onto their two dominating ridges. 185 Brigade was loaned from 3rd Division to help their defence against the inevitable counter-attacks.

Chapter Six

3 & 4 August: XXX Corps

7 Armoured Division was prevented from making further progress by a series of counter attacks. Meanwhile XII Corps, operating with 53 and 59 Division, was closing up to the Villers Bocage-Noyers road and captured Noyers itself together with Missy. NORMANDY TO THE BALTIC

Ondefontaine
43rd Division
130 Brigade
5 Dorset concentrated north of la Bigne during the night of 2/3 August and before dawn resumed their advance through the thick woods on the Ondefontaine road. They spent the whole of the 3rd trying to get through the woods, but were frustrated by fierce resistance from well-hidden machine guns and tanks. 4 Dorset had been attacking southwards from la Bigne with a view to clearing the woods west and south of Ondefontaine. They too ran into heavy fire and suffered severe casualties, but went on to secure their objective. A protracted

A British infantryman operating a captured German MP40 against a sniper.

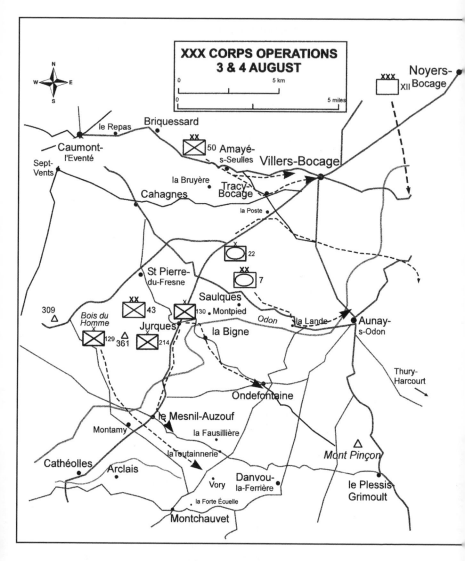

XXX CORPS OPERATIONS
3 & 4 AUGUST

enemy counter-attack was eventually beaten off and the
battalion resumed their earlier position where they came under
heavy mortar and shellfire during the night.

Next day, A Squadron Sherwood Rangers moved towards
Montpied to protect the left flank while 5 Dorset and C
Squadron again advanced through the woods. This time enemy
resistance was weaker and at 1700 hrs 43 Reconnaissance

Regiment reported Ondefontaine clear of enemy. 4 Dorsets moved forward with A Company leading but at 1830 hrs they were stopped by fire from Tiger tanks and machine guns and had to withdraw to dig in for the night on the edge of a wood short of the village. Ondefontaine was heavily mortared and shelled during the night and, at 0500 hrs on the 5th, 4 Dorsets entered the village. They found literally nothing left, the enemy having completely withdrawn during the night.

On 3 August, 7 Hampshire and C Squadron Sherwood Rangers were still held up in Jurques. Another attempt to advance in the small hours had been halted by machine-gun fire and mines. Further attempts throughout the day were frustrated by heavy and accurate mortar and machine-gun fire. However, on the night of 3rd/4th the enemy withdrew and B Company of the Hampshires was able to secure the high ground to the west of the village at dawn on the 4th.

214 Brigade

To the right of 130 Brigade, 5 DCLI had entered Jurques with B Squadron 4/7 Dragoon Guards. They were leading 214 Brigade with orders to clear away the opposition facing 7 Hampshire on the ridge ahead, and exploit in the general direction of Mont Pinçon. The Commanding Officer 5 DCLI sent his carrier platoon forward to determine the extent of the task. They reached Jurques by midnight and groped their way in moonlight through the rubble and craters to the southern exit to the town. A long steep hill lay ahead, and, after they had crossed a bridge across a stream a lone Spandau opened up, but no more was heard until the leading carrier reached the crest of the hill. Then two or three machine guns opened fire; Tiger tanks could be heard starting their engines and flares went up. In a short time two of the three carriers in the leading section had been knocked out. Clearly enemy infantry and tanks held the ridge in strength and the battalion group attacked at 0815. With the support of the divisional artillery they made good progress until some eight to ten, well concealed, Tiger and Panther tanks opened fire on them. They had met 10th SS Panzer Division.

10th SS *Frundsberg* Panzer Division.

B Squadron 4/7 Dragoon Guards now tried to deploy off the road, but found the country on either side to be covered with rocks and ravines. They therefore advanced straight up the hill until a German tank, waiting for them on the crest, knocked out the leading tank. Eventually, although unable to reach it themselves, B Squadron supported their infantry on to their objective. The DCLI held their position there despite enemy mortar fire, which increased 'to a fantastic intensity', but despite substantial artillery support, it became clear that the battalion would make no further progress that day.

1 Worcesters were therefore sent into the thickly wooded country to the right flank and it took the remaining five hours of daylight for their B Company to reach the crest of the ridge, after working through the forest and round the fighting in which 5 DCLI were embroiled.

For their part the DCLI had been probing the tangled gullies on their immediate right. Sergeant Long, with two others of the sniper section, formed one of the patrols trying to find a route. They skilfully worked their way to the summit, much of it on all fours and came across an abandoned farmhouse. There they set up observation from the attic and, suddenly, 'saw five Germans come out of a dug-out and set up a small mortar, oblivious to the fact that they were being closely watched.' Sergeant Long and his two men each shot one of them, the others diving for cover. He then returned to report to his CO, coming back with a portable 38 wireless set. The trio now waited in the attic for dawn. More Germans then exposed themselves to the deadly sniper fire. Then a truck approached at speed; into it the survivors scrambled and hastily made off. All this had been reported over the wireless and soon a DCLI company had occupied the area. They found that Sergeant Long and his two companions had killed eight Germans and had almost certainly

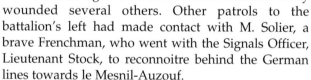

wounded several others. Other patrols to the battalion's left had made contact with M. Solier, a brave Frenchman, who went with the Signals Officer, Lieutenant Stock, to reconnoitre behind the German lines towards le Mesnil-Auzouf.

214 Brigade were now able to push on and 5 DCLI were told to make good the Ondefontaine road and 7 Som LI were sent through 1 Worcesters towards le Mesnil-Auzouf and Montamy.

Reconnaissance
Corps

Ahead of the brigade probed armoured car troops of 43 Reconnaissance Regiment and those of B

Typhoon being bombed up during the fighting in Normandy.

Squadron moved up the steep hill out of Jurques, through the 5 DCLI positions. A passing patrol of RAF Typhoons saw the apparent mêlée of armoured cars, half-tracks and infantry as needing help and dived into the attack. Twenty-four hours earlier it would have been much appreciated. As it was, it was fortunate that only two of the DCLI were wounded.

Two of the troops then made their way along the road to

Ondefontaine, where they came under heavy machine-gun fire. A sharp battle developed in which German tanks made their presence felt – and in which the carrier platoon of 5 DCLI also joined in. Clearly, Ondefontaine had not yet been abandoned.

On the boundaries with VIII Corps, C Squadron of the Reconnaissance Regiment had driven through the Bois du Homme and made their way through le Mesnil-Auzouf. Towards nightfall they reached Montchauvet, la Toutannerie and Vory and encountered the enemy, bringing down small-arms fire and heavy mortaring.

129 Brigade

On 3 August the 13/18 Hussars had been released from 50th Division and reverted to 8 Armoured Brigade and 43rd Division. The regiment concentrated at le Repas, but that evening moved off to join 129 Brigade in the Bois du Homme. As they came into their new harbour area, after a very hot and dusty journey, there was a cloudburst lasting some fifteen minutes. At this stage the plan was for the brigade group to head east and seize crossings over the River Orne south of Thury-Harcourt. That was abandoned for an attack on Mont Pinçon, now in striking distance. 4 Wiltshire were to take the right hand axis, riding on the tanks of B Squadron, 13th/18th, while 5 Wiltshire were carried by A Squadron on the left, followed by 4 Somerset Light Infantry with C Squadron and Regimental Headquarters. By nightfall, after an advance of four miles through the narrow lanes and in dense clouds of white dust, they had reached the vehicles of 43 Reconnaissance Regiment knocked out on the approaches to Montchauvet. The 13/18 Hussars' War Diary recorded their day:

> *0600 Nothing to report. Situation still too unfirm to launch 129 Bde.*
>
> *1500 O Gp held at 129 Bde HQ. The thrust is to be somewhat modified in view of the enemy's disinclination to give up even our start line, and our objective has now been limited to the dominating feature of MONT PINCON. Operation SINAI.*
>
> *1830 "B" Sqn moved to marry up with 4 Wilts to form vanguard of the advance on the Northern Axis.[from le Mesnil-Auzouf]*
>
> *1900 Remainder of Regt moved to join 4 Somersets to move on Southern Axis. Start point is to be Montamy – time 2000 hrs and condition moonlight. The inf are to be carried on our tanks.*

The Som LI were unable to reach the start line by 2000 hrs, but 4 Wilts and B Squadron got under way and travelled about two miles before being held up by an enemy strong point at la Forte Écuelle. By then the southern route had been found to be almost impassable, 'being only a jungle path', and after trying to push on to the level of B Squadron, the remainder of 13/18 Hussars stopped and extricated themselves, and harboured for the night. A Squadron was now placed in support of the reserve battalion, 5 Wilts but were unable to make contact with them until next morning.

Aunay-sur-Odon and Villers-Bocage
7 Armoured and 50th Divisions

The overnight attack by 1/6 Queen's on the high ground two miles west of Aunay-sur-Odon had been successful and by 0400 hrs on 3 August the position was cleared of enemy. The three companies astride the main road east of Saulques were joined at dawn by 5 RTR and the advance continued, led by B Squadron 5 RTR through thick mist. When that lifted, at about 0830 hrs, their leading troop was attacked near la Lande. The squadron was soon sharply engaged in la Lande itself and lost four tanks, knocking out four of the enemy's. During the afternoon fierce counter-attacks were made by the Germans on 6 Queens' positions and at one stage two squadrons of the 5 RTR were cut off and some of the company positions were overrun. One of the 8 Hussars' squadrons drove off the enemy, but the two squadrons of 5 RTR were still cut off. By the time that they broke out, after dark, they had lost an officer and six men killed, four other officers and twenty men wounded and eight men missing; seven Cromwells had been destroyed. However, they had taken forty prisoners. In 6 Queen's there were 135 casualties, of whom seven were officers, while the

'Desert Rat' of 7th Armoured Division

'Double T' of 50th Northumbrian Division

Norfolk Yeomanry lost thirty and had three anti-tank guns destroyed.

While that battle was going on, the Inniskilling Dragoon Guards had found Tracy Bocage to be still strongly held and it was left to 50th Division to take it after securing Amayé. Having

Villers-Bocage 'reduced to rubble by the RAF'.

captured the town, 50th Division endured twenty-four hours of shelling, both on that position and the Amayé feature.

By now Villers-Bocage had become a household word in Britain as press and wireless reported the attacks on it, both by land and from the air. But, helped by the pressure being applied on the left by 59th Division of XII Corps, 50th Division seized it at last. On the morning of 4 August, 1 Dorset underwent a barrage that was to be the final enemy 'Hate'.

From 7th Armoured Division, the 11 Hussars eventually managed to find a way through Villers-Bocage, reduced to rubble by the RAF and littered with mines. With the help of the flails of the Westminster Dragoons they reached the outskirts of the town by evening and made way for the Inniskillings and a Rifle Brigade company to pass through. Following up were patrols from 1 Dorset of 50th Division. They moved forward, taking a number of prisoners, and in the afternoon one of them reached the outskirts of Villers-Bocage. They too found a scene of 'utter carnage'. Each street had been razed to the ground and was littered by knocked out tanks and trucks. Since the brief capture by 7th Armoured Division in June there had been weeks of pounding from the air and from Allied guns.

Meanwhile, 22 Armoured Brigade, with 5 Queen's under command, was sent after dark in a cross-country loop to the left, via la Poste, in the hope of being able to by-pass Aunay to the north and gain the high ground beyond.

German Withdrawal

On orders from Hitler, the Germans were now preparing for the attack by Seventh Army on the Mortain salient. In order to cover the flanks and rear of the planned attack, the commander of Fifth Panzer Army, Eberbach, had decided to abandon the ruins of Villers-Bocage, Aunay and Evrécy. During 4 and 5 August his troops were withdrawing to the Orne, covering their retreat with mines, booby-traps and demolitions. Their plan was to hold fast along the line from Bourguébus Ridge to Vire, via the Orne, Thury-Harcourt – and Mont Pinçon.

Chapter Seven

3 & 4 August: VIII Corps

Heavy fighting continued on 3 August; south of the Vire-Vassy road 11 Armoured Division was engaged with strong enemy forces, while the Guards continued to be heavily engaged round Estry. NORMANDY TO THE BALTIC

The opposition that the BLUECOAT divisions were encountering was itself a measure of the success of the operation so far: '... Already, however, Operation BLUECOAT had amply fulfilled its purpose. By its swift advance to the Vire-Vassy road VIII Corps had intercepted the armoured reinforcements which had been destined for Seventh Army.' But the price was high; of the two hundred tanks destroyed over the past four days, two thirds were British, while the infantry were continuing to take heavy losses. 3rd Division now backed up 11th Armoured Division, heavily

Troops and armour advancing along the main Vassy road on 4 August 1944.

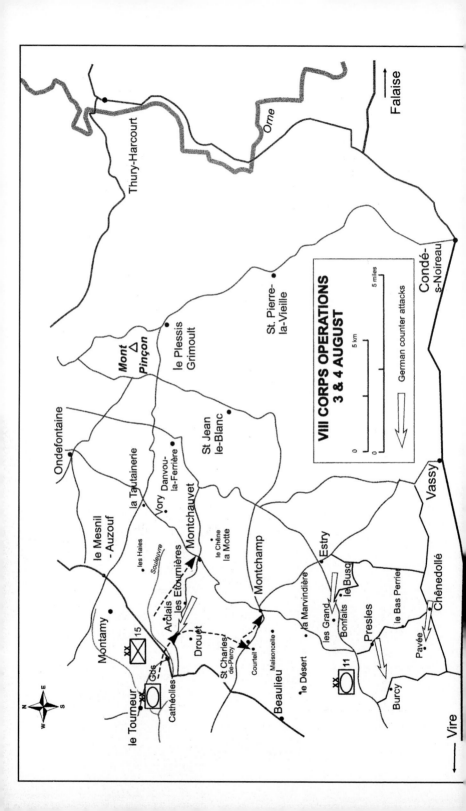

engaged south of the Vire-Vassy road and 15th Division were backing up Guards Armoured, to whom 44 Brigade was detached during 3 August.

Arclais, Maisoncelles and Montchamp
Guards Armoured Division

On 3 August, Guards Armoured Division were fighting round Arclais, overlooking Cathéolles. 44 Brigade plus the Seaforth had moved up near le Tourneur and were given the task of clearing the two ridges on the north and south banks of the Souleuvre east of Cathéolles. The plan was for the Royal Scots Fusiliers, with a squadron of 4 Grenadiers, to take the northern ridge of Arclais during that afternoon. The long, narrow ridge is steep-sided and wooded - and scored with ravines. On the approach there is a tributary of the Souleuvre, across which the bridges were broken. It was 2100 hrs before the attack could begin and, in the fading light, all but four of the Grenadiers' tanks were bogged down.

L/Sgt. Davies's tank was bogged so deep that the water came into his turret. The enemy fired a bazooka at it, then surrounded it and told the

A Sherman on the main Vassy road, 4 August 1944.

crew to surrender. To this there was only one answer given somewhat crudely by Gdsm. Norgrove, and accompanied by a round of 75. The enemy tried to open the engine doors but luckily they were locked and the crew remained in the tank, half full of water, until dawn.

Meanwhile the remaining four tanks could still give the RSF valuable support as they carried on up the slopes and across the ridge to les Haies. By 1030 hrs they were on the high ground overlooking Montchauvet.

Next day the ridge south of the Souleuvre was tackled. On it there were four or five 'large rectangular coverts', in which enemy guns and mortars had been active. The Royal Scots and KOSB advanced east through 1 Welsh Guards, scaling en route an almost perpendicular bluff. However, they met little opposition and, by 0900 hrs, were on their objective – the road from Montchamp to Montchauvet – having taken a number of prisoners from 9th SS Panzer Division. 44 Brigade then reverted to command of 15th Division.

The clearance by 44 Brigade's advance gave considerable relief over the wide area that the German observation posts had

A Bren gunner of the Guards during the advance.

dominated. By midday the road from Montchauvet to Montchamp had been cut and, advancing along the ridge, 3 Irish Guards captured much of Maisoncelles in the morning.

As soon as the division's hold on the ridge was consolidated, 1 Welsh Guards were told to turn right and descend to Montchamp. After taking it in a hard fight they were repeatedly counter-attacked by troops from 9th SS Panzer Division.

With 5 Guards Brigade split across the high ground of Arclais, Drouet and la Marvindière 32 Guards Brigade were required to force a way through to Montchamp and Estry. 3 Irish Guards were to undertake this, supported by a squadron of Coldstream tanks, while 1 Welsh Guards moved up to south of the Cathéolles bridge in reserve. When they arrived there were still Germans within six hundred yards who put in a small counter-attack, but they withdrew during the night. It took the Irish Guards most of an unpleasant day to make their way on foot to St Charles-de-Percy along a road littered with dead horses and destroyed transport and under almost continuous shelling. Immediately on arrival an attack was launched on the small village of Courteil immediately south-east of St Charles-de-Percy. It was dark by the time it was captured it was dark and the larger village of Maisoncelles had to wait until next day.

To the north-east, three determined counter-attacks had been made against the Grenadier group and the Germans obviously intended to recapture, not only the spur which they held, but also the Cathéolles bridge. From their slightly higher ridge to the east the Germans had all round observation and they had to be moved off as soon as possible. Bypassing was not feasible, as further reinforcements in the shape of 9th SS Panzer Division had now arrived. The steep and thickly wooded slopes made it essentially a task for infantry. Fortunately 15th Division could now be spared from some of its task of flank protection, and 44 Brigade was provided for the operation, plus 1 Welsh Guards as a fourth battalion.

9th SS *Hohenstaufen* Panzer Division.

11th Armoured Division

On 3 August the expected German counter-attacks came in on 11th Armoured Division – 9th SS Panzer Division were pushing hard against the Estry and Perrier ridges. The small village of Presles, between the two ridges, was recaptured and heavy attacks came in all along the line. On the left, 4 KSLI and 3 RTR clung on to their position at les Grand Bonfaits against determined tank and infantry attacks from le Busq. Further west 3 Mons, with 2 Fife and Forfar, were dug in around Pavée.

8 Rifle Brigade and 23 Hussars were cut off for twenty-four hours during which the mounting casualties could not be evacuated. Further counter-attacks came in from the woods to the south of the 8 Rifle Brigade group position during the afternoon of 4 August, together with heavy mortar fire. The 23 Hussars reinforced the artillery's defensive fire tasks by blasting the woods with HE shells and the Germans fell back to le Bas Perrier. There was a repeat performance in the evening. The 23 Hussars were isolated again for a while and the divisional supply route broken but a supply column of ammunition managed to arrive safely.

Chênedollé, as the obvious concentration point for the Germans was shelled, but the Ayrshire Yeomanry had two FOOs wounded in the fighting over Burcy, which was taken and retaken. The Perrier ridge positions were still cut off, but 4 KSLI had 'a relatively peaceful day' while on the right 3 RTR with a battery from 77 Anti Tank Regiment had a successful conclusion to a day of heavy shelling and mortaring, destroying two Panthers, one Tiger and a SP gun.

15th Division

During the afternoon of 4 August, the Royal Scots Fusiliers, with a squadron of 4 Grenadiers, cleared Montchauvet and made contact with 43rd Division coming from the north.

After being relieved by 46 Brigade the Royal Scots and the KOSB cleared the remainder of the southern ridge up to la Motte in the east. The attack began after dark, lit by blazing houses and hayricks in Montchauvet and Montchamp and it took all night to move their vehicles and SP anti-tank guns along hill tracks and under heavy mortar fire. The later stages of the advance, fortunately hidden by mist, were not completed until next morning.

Chapter Eight

'Converging' on Mont Piçon – 5 August

'... 43 Division continued to converge on Mont Pinçon ...'
NORMANDY TO THE BALTIC

The Formidable Obstacle

Mont Pinçon rises only some 1,200 feet from the *bocage*, but it is the highest hill in Normandy and it completely dominates the whole landscape from Vire to the Odon.

> *From its slopes German observation was uninterrupted and the enemy were able to bring down deadly artillery and mortar fire on any movement. The crest is a plateau covered with heather and bracken interspersed with a few birch trees. The higher slopes are well wooded and very steep on the southern and south-western sides. Small fields, divided by thick hedges, stretch down the lower slopes towards the stream at the foot which is in full view from the top. La Varinière and le Quesnée are typical bocage villages, strongly built of stone, surrounded by orchards and intersected by a labyrinth of sunken lanes and stout walls. The enemy's strong resistance here and the evil reputation which the cross-roads at la Varinière were to gain, even after Mont Pinçon had fallen, will therefore be readily understood.* (43rd Wessex Division at War)

General Thomas's plan for 5 August was for 129 Brigade to assault Mont Pinçon from the west and south-west, via la Varinière and St Jean-le-Blanc. Information on the defenders was scant; BLUECOAT had played havoc with the formations and units of Fifth Panzer Army, but known to have been in the area were elements of 276th and 326th Infantry Divisions, 21st and 9th SS Panzer Divisions. As in the Russian campaigns, the Germans speedily put together effective ad hoc groupings from the remnants of shattered formations and units.

At 0800 hrs on 5 August, from their overnight halt near la Forte Écuelle, 4 Wilts and B Squadron 13/18 Hussars resumed their advance. A Squadron were to move on a parallel route to the north carrying 5 Wilts.

> *'B' Squadron on the go quite early but these lanes and roads are such that speed is out of the question; it is far more a question of whether you can move at all and this doesn't consider enemy mines at all...so off we*

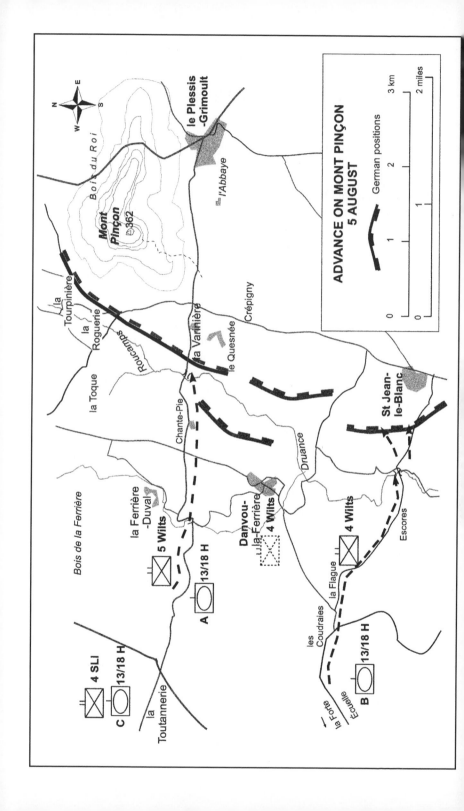

go now on three routes, 'A' north, 'B' centre, and 'C' behind 'B' all out for Mt. Pinçon.

Frightful chaos on the way as we ran into15th Scottish Division – held us up an hour.

Very little comic relief today except the refugees returning with donkey-drawn carts. The donkeys reacted exactly as you'd expect when tanks are milling about. Fortunately there was no stonking on at the time and it was one of the few times today I have been able to poke my head out. **(War Diary of Julius Neave)**

St Jean-le-Blanc
4 Wiltshire and B Squadron 13/18 Hussars

After la Forte Écuelle no further opposition was encountered by the 4 Wiltshire group as they approached St Jean-le-Blanc, via les Coudraies and la Flague until just after passing Escores. The road then descended to cross the Druance stream. Today it may seem extraordinary that such a small stream could have proved

such an obstacle in 1944. They found that the bridge had been blown and that the banks of the stream were mined. C Company waded through it and up the steep, wooded slopes beyond. They found themselves at close grips with a well-concealed and determined enemy. A desperate battle then began which was to last all day.

C Company commander was Major 'Dim' Robbins:

The bridge, which we had expected to cross, was blown. My commanding officer said 'the orders are to get on, let the tanks stay here for now. Continue on foot to that river and get across to the village, which is only a mile or two.' Once we got into the

Major 'Dim' Robbins, 4 Wiltshire.

rougher ground, getting higher and higher, it was very steep, very hot and sporadic fire broke out. The battle lasted for several hours because of the close nature of it. Every time we tried to advance - it drew very heavy fire.

There were a lot of inter-section battles, almost hand-to-hand battles, for buildings, for a bit of area. The right platoon had all three section commanders, corporals, knocked out - wounded or killed. The platoon was commanded by then by a Lance Corporal. He was a battalion boxer, called Jenkins. He had given me a lot of trouble, but he was an

95

excellent fellow! I remember him leading a small counter attack and meeting head on with a German doing the same thing with about ten men. It was fascinating to watch as Jenkins won. This was going on the whole time; that platoon was knocked out practically, but it stayed. On the left there was similar fighting and this went on all day.

The Battalion Mortar Platoon, under Captain Tom Powell, had been sent forward to help: 'I went off to support C Company who were having a real tough time. I think I fired a couple of thousand bombs – we had unlimited ammunition.' In the meantime the Pioneer Platoon, despite heavy mortar and *Nebelwerfer* fire, had been putting together a new bridge and over it, at about 1600 hrs, passed a troop of B Squadron tanks to help the hard-pressed company across the stream. Another company advanced on St Jean-le-Blanc. Well-entrenched infantry supported by tanks opposed them, 'who fought to a finish amongst the orchards and corn fields'. 'Dim' Robbins:

Captain John Fletcher, 94 Field Regiment RA.

It took us two hours to finish the battle and capture the place. There were a lot of casualties – on both sides. No Germans surrendered. They fought to the end and clearly must have been a rearguard company set with that task. By 1800 hours they had all been shot or had withdrawn and there we were, Germans lying about dead, ourselves lying about wounded and dead. ...

I had a very good Forward Observation Officer of 94th Field Regiment, Captain John Fletcher. He and I went forward, while the men were digging themselves in, to get a suitable OP for him, because clearly the Germans had gone on down the hill. And as we came to a further ridge, round the corner of a field, we bumped head on into two Germans, sentries, armed with Schmeissers. I of course was far too slow to do anything about it, but the Gunner reacted – as any good infantryman should! and shot the first chap; the other one may have been wounded, but he legged it down the hill and away.

We looked down the hill and there was at least a company of Germans, with tanks, forming up to carry out the natural thing after a

The Druance stream.

battle – make a counter attack. Young Fletcher got on to his Regiment; and before you could say 'knife' – well, in a few minutes – a stonk came down – heavy artillery – on these people which dispersed them. It was a shock to find the battle was by no means over. I went back and night was falling. The troop of tanks withdrew for – whatever they do at night! So we were left in this rather eerie position digging in, Germans quite close, no grub, and waited. We did not quite know what to do next except to defend the place.

Corporal Nevill Trim of 4 Wiltshires was left with the impression: 'There was so much going on all the time. We just took one day at a time. We used to wake up in the morning and think, "Oh good gosh I'm still here".'

By early evening the whole battalion was across the Druance, but it was clear that St Jean-le-Blanc was too strongly held. They were withdrawn after dark. At about 2100 hrs 'Dim' Robbins was told that: it had been decided by the brigade commander that 4 Wilts should withdraw, because the objective was Mont Pinçon, not St Jean-le-Blanc, and he had decided on a different way.

The cost of that little battle for that day was one officer and twenty-one other ranks killed, two officers and thirty-seven other ranks

Approaching the bridge at St-Jean-le Blanc.

The bridge today.

wounded and, with depleted companies, that's a lot.

Chante-Pie and the bridge over the Druance
5 Wiltshire and A Squadron 13/18 Hussars

At 1100 hrs on the 5th, A Squadron had been ordered to rendezvous at la Toutannerie with 5 Wilts who were moving across country.

> '... it was not known what enemy might be encountered en route to this new RV. Enemy encountered but they were found to be gunners coming into action. This caused some delay.'

After meeting up, 5 Wiltshires were carried to the cross roads near la Ferrière-Duval. Hugh Elliot, troop leader in A Squadron, carried a whole company of 5 Wilts on his tanks:

> '... Men plus equipment, 25-30 to a tank. APCs were just a pipe dream at this time, except for the motor battalions... fortunately we were not shot at and didn't lose any on the way.'

After A Company of the Wiltshires had secured the crossroads:

> The plan now was for the 5 Wilts supported by 'A' Sqn. to move to Mont Pinçon via Chante Pie and la Varinière. There were two wooded ravines (ditches) between us and our objective, both being tank obstacles. The first lay some 2000 yards to the east of the RV and the second about 2000 yds further on. Mont Pinçon was a further 2000 yards beyond second ditch. It was a dominating feature on the left of the road along which we were to advance.

Their first task was to secure the bridge over the Druance, between Chante-Pie and la Varinière – one of the 'ditches' – and the second was la Varinière itself. The third task was the capture of Mont Pinçon, the brigade objective, and for that 5 Wilts would be on the right flank with the Som LI on their left.

Lance Corporal 'Gloves' Garner, 5 Wiltshire.

Over the next two days the bridge, which no longer exists as such, and the surrounding ground were to be the scene of the fiercest fighting in the battle for Mont Pinçon. At 1300 hrs the advance towards it began with a left flanking move by D Company. 18 Platoon led the way across the fields to the north

German troops moving through a village.

of the crossroads and reached some farm buildings. There they found a 'very suspicious' French woman who they thought might have had something to do with the amazing accuracy of the German shelling. Lance Corporal 'Gloves' Garner of 5 Wiltshire remembers the encounter:

> There was a lot of mortar fire coming down on us and, while we were getting there, there was a report came from one of the companies that they had found a woman in a German trench and she wouldn't come out. I was detailed with a sergeant to see what this woman was doing. She was about forty years old and had an Alsatian dog with her. We were worried that she might have been put out there to inform the enemy what we were doing. We got her out of the trench and she had this sort of sack on her back; and, of course, it was about a dozen pairs of shoes!

18 Platoon then came under fire from a small wood. Sergeant King, the Platoon Sergeant, was wounded but, when the wood was occupied, only two German stretcher-bearers were found.

They were made to carry Sergeant King to the Regimental Aid Post and, on the way back the party came under fire. One of the German stretcher-bearers saved Sergeant King's life by diving on top of him and receiving a bullet in his own back. The platoon pushed on across the stream and through the wood on the far side, followed by 16 Platoon. To the south of the road, however, 17 Platoon, were pinned down in a cornfield by machine-gun fire. From the troop of A Squadron supporting the company one of the tank commanders spotted where the fire was coming from, on the other side of the stream, and, firing over the heads of 17 Platoon, quickly dealt with it. Then came down a heavy mortar barrage, but in a few minutes the platoon

German patrol checking out a French farm.

was across the stream and beginning to dig in just forward of a narrow wood. By now 18 Platoon was about a quarter of a mile beyond the bridge; there they too dug in, as did 16 Platoon. D Company was therefore well placed forward of the bridge, having successfully infiltrated enemy lines.

However, the bridge itself was still very much in enemy hands, despite two direct assaults by C Company under Major Field. Each time they had been beaten back with heavy casualties by a strong and determined defence. Without reconnaissance it would be wholly impracticable to mount a further attack, in darkness, to support D Company. The remaining companies formed into a defensive position around the cross-roads. In Battalion Headquarters was the Adjutant, Captain Harry Peace:

> At battalion HQ we were making for a farmhouse, which was about a mile from the stream, perhaps three quarters of a mile short of the stream. When the rest of Rear Headquarters came up sadly a mortar shell fell on us and killed our much beloved padre, Jimmy Douglas, the cook, 'Double' Davies, and several others. Not exactly a good start to a battle. Dusk was falling and there we were, Germans and ourselves seemed to be mixed up; one company across the river – and that was the situation.

Captain Lyon's successor as A Squadron second-in-command was Captain Noel Denny:

> The Squadron sat about 200 yards short of the stream, which ran across the front, from six until dusk and were shelled almost continually. The infantry suffered heavy casualties. It was not until we got on top of the mountain and looked back to where we had been sitting that we discovered that our position must have been clearly seen by any number of German artillery forward observing officers, although we thought we were well covered by a huge treed hedge. We were very lucky not to have any casualties.

It was now pitch dark and 'determined and fanatical' Germans

Men of the Wiltshire Regiment walking past signs warning of mines on the verges.

surrounded D Company Periodically an enemy patrol ran through the position, firing as they went. In what was clearly a desperate situation, the company commander set off to report to Battalion HQ, taking only a runner with him – who was killed on the way.

> *During the course of the night Mickey Thomas, the very gallant commander of D Company, had got across the stream and worked his way back through the enemy to tell us that his company had infiltrated right into the heart of an enemy position. He was totally surrounded and inevitably would be destroyed. There was no way in which one could get help for him in the middle of the night so he was given permission to withdraw and he went back to his company.*

It was 0400 hrs when Major Thomas reached his company again and they began the nightmare process of withdrawal. In single file they went through the dark along the road towards the bridge:

> *... and all went well until close to the bridge a guttural voice ordered 'Halt'. Major Thomas, shouting 'Duck!' made a dash for the other side of the road, but he fell riddled with machine-gun bullets. Pandemonium broke loose; the air was full with the rattle of machine-guns; and the Company scattered on either side of the road, many of the men taking*

advantage of the cover afforded by the steep banks of the stream.

Most of 18 Platoon went to the right and, led by Sergeant Titcombe along the bed of the stream, got back to where they had crossed it before. They could then retrace their steps to the battalion. 16 Platoon had scattered to the left of the road with enemy between them and the only other route they knew. Sergeant Latton told his NCOs each to take a group of men and make their own way back independently. After a variety of adventures they were soon back 'in comparative safety'.

Lieutenant Slater's Platoon was also cut off and split in two halves. The Platoon Sergeant, Sergeant Witherone, with one half and some stragglers from other platoons, took the route to the left and they too successfully reached the battalion position, 'chiefly owing to the fine leadership of Sergeant Witherone'. Lieutenant Slater, with the other half, took the right of the road. They reached the wood, where Sergeant King had been wounded the night before, and through which most of 16 and 18 Platoons had already passed. But now the enemy had the wood covered and they were surrounded; any move brought fire. They lay there for many hours during which two volunteers tried to get back to the battalion; one was killed but the other got through. Nevertheless, it was the following night before Lieutenant Slater and his few remaining men could get back to safety. The company had only thirty-eight survivors.

13/18 Hussars

At dusk, A and B Squadrons of the 13th/18th harboured with their Regimental Headquarters west of Chante-Pie crossroads. In the Commanding Officer's tank the Adjutant wrote up his diary for the day:

> ... on all routes we were held up on the line west of St Jean le Blanc and Mt. Pinçon. We have been scrapping all day to sort these routes out, but the old game of spandaus and mortars has started again and little progress is made.
>
> RHQ sitting back about a mile and a half got a smart shelling several times but fortunately only one slight casualty
>
> I find sitting in the tank for hours on end in this weather very trying but suppose it might be much worse. Our Boche prisoners all reckon it's absolute hell, this war, and some taken today reckon that but for what they describe as the 'sod of an officer' they would have given themselves up long ago. But at any rate for the moment they're fighting hard....

There is little doubt he doesn't mean us to get past the river today and St Jean le Blanc is strongly held.

We had a very smart shelling just before nightfall which was much too close – we didn't have any casualties ourselves – but others did and there were some rather unpleasant sights.

I went to check-up on casualties and on my rounds found amongst 'other' things a hutch full of about 20 starving tame rabbits. Like a bloody fool I chucked them bunches of grass and went off. Why I didn't let them out, God knows.

About midnight we withdrew from the river line to leaguer a little north of our position during the day – also much stonked. We had to pick up our infantry and drop them in Danvou. There was considerable argument as to whether in fact the area is clear of enemy or not. However the shelling was the only trouble our harbourers had!

4 Wiltshire

But 4 Wiltshire had an uncomfortable night:

Regrettably this concentration area, when dawn broke, was in full view of the enemy. They were in Danvou, or had OPs in Danvou, and while we were at last having an early breakfast, they shattered us with very heavy artillery and mortar fire. During this ten-minute shelling, D Company lost one officer and nine men killed and two officers and twenty-seven men wounded. (Later that day the Company went into the attack with one officer and 58 men.)

We were then given our orders to go much further left to take up position as brigade reserve behind 4th Somerset Light Infantry who were miles away. [Robbins]

Captain Tom Powell, 4 Wiltshire.

We stayed overnight; we dug in as best we could. Some dug in, and some didn't. Next morning when we were going to have breakfast, and it was getting misty, they started sending the flipping shells over. It was a bit dicey then. [Trim]

A lot of men in the companies were killed. I had three or four casualties in the Mortar Platoon. It was a bad pitch there. I do not want to be shot by the brigade major of the time if he is still alive but it wasn't a very clever move. [Powell]

C *Squadron 13/18 Hussars*

At 1000hrs C Squadron and RHQ 13/18 Hussars, had moved off carrying 4 Som LI on the northern route, before returning to the southern one. At 1030 C Squadron reported 'considerable congestion on road caused by Guards Tank Bde. This was cleared up for a time but they soon appeared again and it was necessary to give up Southern axis and move in rear of B Sqn.'. C Squadron finally harboured for the night just north of Danvou where they too experienced how exposed it was to enemy fire:

The following morning the harbour area was heavily shelled and SSM Park was mortally wounded. Tpr Hadwin was also killed and Pte. Williams (ACC) seriously wounded.

Chapter Nine

'A Footing' – 6 August

On 30 Corps front 43 Division gained a footing on Mont Pinçon after severe fighting. Normandy to the Baltic

Ambitious Plans

At 1300 hrs on 5 August XXX Corps had issued ambitious orders on the operations for the 6th. 43rd Division was to complete the capture of Mont Pinçon by 1000 hrs and advance with 7th Armoured Division due south on Condé-sur-Noireau, nine miles further on. At that stage 7th Armoured was only just entering Aunay.

The Sherwood Rangers War Diary for 6 August filled in some background:

> 8 Armd Bde Gp with 214 Bde (43 Div) are to take part in Operation BLACKWATER the objective of which is CONDE-SUR-NOIREAU (5732) 15 miles to the South. During first phase of op 4/7 DG are lead and the general object is to go round strong enemy defences rather than to sit and fight a pitched battle. Everything was teed up for us to move at night but after we had formed up the whole Op was called off consequent upon 4/7 DG encountering strong opposition soon after they had crossed the start line. The capture of MT. PINCON by others of our tps was to have been a necessary preliminary to the launching of BLACKWATER. MT. PINCON was still in enemy hands.

Meanwhile General Thomas's revised plan of attack on Mont Pinçon was for 130 Brigade to make a feint attack from the north while 129 Brigade struck from the west. This meant assaulting the steepest slope of the hill, but there was no time to work troops round to the north where the incline was less: 'The new Corps Commander (Lieutenant General Horrocks) was a man of fire and he had orders to capture Mont Pinçon without delay.'

Feint by 130 Brigade

7 Hampshire led the 130 Brigade attack with objectives of Plecière, Roucamps, and le Postil. It began at 1100 hrs, with C Company on the right and D Company on the left. The first bound was reached without great difficulty and B Company passed through D to reach Plecière and secure it despite heavy

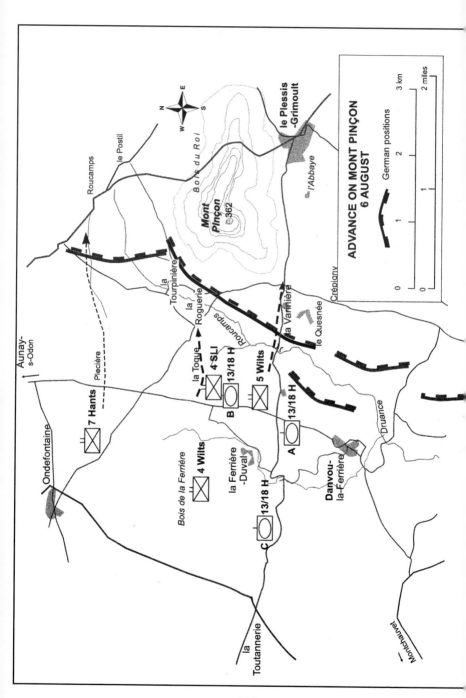

ADVANCE ON MONT PINÇON
6 AUGUST

German positions

0   1   2   3 km
0   1   2 miles

mortar fire. On the left, however, A Company came under heavy machine-gun fire as they advanced towards. The severe casualties included the company commander, Captain Wright and the company was withdrawn behind D Company. An attempt was then made to go round the opposition, crossing a stream to the south of Plecière, while 112 Field Regiment RA engaged Roucamps. C Company came up on the left of B and at 1400 hrs both companies advanced. They were at once held up by heavy machine-gun fire from the opposite side of the stream and from Roucamps itself. However, a Canadian officer of B Company, Lieutenant Taylor, (a number of Canadian officers were serving in 43rd Division) managed to cross the stream with one section. He led them right forward to an enemy machine-gun post and, before the crew could withdraw, Taylor killed two of them and captured the other two. The rest of B Company was still held up by enemy fire so he had to withdraw, taking his two prisoners with him. C Company had also taken heavy casualties, including all their officers. It was apparent that no further progress could be made and both companies were withdrawn. With a view to making a further attack in the evening, an artillery bombardment was put in hand.

129 Brigade's Second Assault

Throughout the night of the 5th, planning for the next day had gone on in 129 Brigade, followed next morning by 'O' Groups and reconnaissance under heavy fire. 5 Wiltshire, with A Squadron 13/18 Hussars, were to attack on the line of the road through the la Varinière crossroads to the south-west of the mountain. On the left, 4 Somerset Light Infantry were to tackle the high ground on the eastern edge of the hill, where the terrain was considered impassable to tanks. Their axis was to be the road from la Toque to la Roguerie and on to Pt. 362. 4 Wiltshire and B and C Squadrons 13th/18th were in reserve.

In one of the battalion 'O' Groups:

> ... the Commanding Officer of 5th Wiltshire was giving out his orders for the attack on Mont Pinçon by his battalion supported by A Squadron. At 11 o'clock the right-hand company supported by Lieutenant Elliot's troop was counter-attacked and Major Wormald left the battalion commander's order group to go out and deal with this nuisance... necessitated postponing H Hour from noon till two

109

o'clock.'

'The Squadron Leader came back to the harbour area to give out orders, but, as he came into the corner of the field and blew the inevitable whistle for crew commanders ["TL" for Troop Leaders and "CC" for Crew Commanders - in Morse], a heavy 'stonk' came down and held up proceedings for a few minutes. Eventually the 'O' Group formed up in a sunken road, with each person sitting in a slit trench and the Squadron Leader shouting at the top of his voice to make himself heard above the noise of the shells passing overhead. He walked up and down, apparently unconcerned.'

Major Wormald:

...we did not know for certain whether the bridge had been cleared of mines... We also knew that the river/stream was in a wooded ravine and that it was an obstacle to tanks. The plan was that as soon as the infantry had established a bridgehead the Squadron would cross the bridge, deploy and lead the infantry into la Varinière, following up an artillery barrage.

4 Somerset Light Infantry

4 Som LI were carried into battle mounted on the tanks of B Squadron 13/18 Hussars. Amongst them was Corporal Douglas Proctor...

... tank tracks were swirling up the dust. If the Germans didn't

'We could hardly breathe; all we could do was to hang on the backs of the tanks.'

Lieutenant Sydney Jary, 4 Somerset Light Infantry.

know we were preparing for an attack they did once we started moving. There was a terrific cloud of dust it must have been seen for twenty miles. We could hardly breath; all we could do was cling on the banks of the tanks and hope we'd soon get to Duval – that was the concentration area; the start line.

His new platoon commander, Sydney Jary wrote:

In England, it was August Bank Holiday. In Nottingham, Corporal Proctor's wife, Jean, was due to bear their first child. In Normandy, Mont Pinçon loomed above us menacingly. Here would be my first battle in command of 18 Platoon.

The Battalion "0" Group took place at 1230 hours on that Bank Holiday Monday, 6th August. We were to attack this rugged hill from the west with the 5th Wiltshires on our right and the 4th Wiltshires in reserve. The approach march to our forming up place had been a nightmare of swirling, abrasive dust, shelling and the stench of exhaust fumes from the tanks which transported us forward. We were due to attack at 1500 hours with "A" Company leading on the right and "B" Company on the left. We followed "B" Company.

The ground before us descended to a small stream at the foot of Mont Pinçon and then rose steeply through typical bocage fields with thick hedgerows to a thickly wooded area. The top of the hill was open and crowned with gorse. Inspection through binoculars failed to reveal the existence of any Germans.

4 Som LI were ordered to advance in the direction of Pt 362 and the high ground on the northern side of Mont Pinçon, keeping to the north of la Toque and la Roguerie. They moved up along a narrow and sunken lane followed by 4 Wiltshire. It was swelteringly hot and the Som LI were in shirtsleeves.

"B" Company moved off quickly with our Company deployed about three hundred yards behind. Their forward platoons had barely crossed the stream when concentrated Spandau fire came from the front and from both flanks. There must have been about twelve machine guns firing at one time. This devastating display of firepower stopped the

Battalion dead in its tracks. There was no way forward or round it and no way to retire. Some of the guns had engaged "D" Company over the heads of "B" Company and Private Morris in 18 Platoon was killed.

Powerless and crouching in a hedgerow, I tried to identify the Spandau positions. This proved impossible as they still kept up their crushing display of firepower. In my ignorance I expected that the enemy machine gunners would soon expend their ammunition. They did not. Nor did they in dozens of subsequent battles.

The double-banked hedges provided thick cover that made it easy for the enemy to move unseen from one firing position to another. The Som LI found it impossible to locate a single automatic weapon, although one or more had opened up at varying ranges. Lieutenant Jary put his binoculars to his eyes:

The fire was coming off the hill but I could not locate one gun and I do not know to this day where any of them were. I don't think we yet understood that you cannot attack up a long forward slope in broad daylight to an enemy, who is well dug in, totally invisible and with

British soldier with Sten gun.

great fire power. We should have learned the lesson on 112 but we did it
again. It foundered. The officer commanding B Company was killed.
The forward companies were just about level with the stream.

Looking up Mont Pinçon from la Roguerie one can well
appreciate the plight of Douglas Proctor and his fellow light
infantrymen that summer's afternoon:

3 o'clock was the zero hour when the barrage started and the first
two companies started advancing. We followed a little way behind. The
enemy waited until all the battalion was exposed, every man jack of us,
then they opened up with about a dozen Spandaus strategically placed
all over the hillside and we couldn't spot them at all. All we could do
was hug the ground. We hugged the ground for five or six hours. That's
all we could do; any attempt at moving and a hail of bullets came over
our heads.

With the leading troops of the Som LI was a Forward
Observation Officer, Captain Clarke, from 94 Field Regiment
RA. When the infantry went to ground, Clarke crept forward
from his carrier with Bombardier Eveleigh. He then shouted fire
orders back through Eveleigh to Bombardier Bell in the carrier
and was able to shoot up two machine guns and to keep enemy
heads down generally. But the enemy soon began to use heavy
mortars and 105 mm guns and a mortar bomb fatally wounded
Bell.

5 Wiltshire and A Squadron 13/18 Hussars

5 Wiltshire were to resume their advance and attack the
bridge that they had failed to take the previous day. Captain
Peace said:

We had reformed into two companies – that's all we had the strength
for. We did have a number of sappers, I remember, because of the mines
and we also had the support of the 13/18th Hussars. They were splendid
chaps; they were prepared to lead us into battle and not every tank
squadron was prepared to do that. What with the mist and one thing
and another the start of the attack was delayed until about 2 o'clock,
maybe 2.30. It started with the usual artillery barrage:

The axis for the battalion was that of the previous day – the road
towards le Plessis Grimoult and Mont Pinçon. The companies had
barely crossed the start line when mortar and shellfire crashed down,
while machine-gun fire and snipers opened up from the roadside
orchards. Supporting tanks of the 13/18 Hussars responded with
suppressive fire as they led the way across the open ground on the

left of the road, but men of the Wiltshires on the right came under fire from every possible weapon as they made their way down the slope and towards the stream by way of an orchard. 'Some dashed forward and took cover behind a high bank; some, led by Corporal H. K. Mackrell, ran across the road to the left, close by the bridge itself, and took cover in the bed of the stream.'

As one of Hugh Elliot's tank commanders, Corporal Hammond, approached the bridge the enemy tried to demolish it; but this was not successful. Lance Corporal Hennessey was commanding another of the Shermans in the troop:

> . . . we had fought our way to the foot of the hill against very heavy machine gun and mortar fire, which was taking a steady toll of the infantry. The day was hot and sultry and the air was laden with dust and the stench of dead cattle. Every movement of a vehicle stirred up more dust, which drew more fire from the enemy and curses from the infantry, who lay in shallow slit trenches waiting word to move across the river and up the steep scarp. The pioneers were working to clear the mines on the bridge under cover of a smoke screen and in the face of considerable enemy fire. As soon as the bridge was clear, our artillery put down a barrage on the far bank and we went across the bridge in tanks with the infantry following. They had got about half way when the enemy came to life with machine guns and mortars, catching them in the open. Within minutes the two leading companies were practically wiped out.

During the bitter advance one of the Wiltshire company commanders, Major Milne, trying to set an example, got too far ahead of his men and was taken prisoner only to reappear later. Moving along the road was forward Battalion HQ of 5 Wiltshire in a carrier and a scout car:

It was then that Lieutenant Colonel J. H. C. Pearson, realising that his men were pinned down, got out of his carrier and walked back to tell the Adjutant that he was going ahead on foot to see what the position was and to urge the men forward. He added with a grin: 'I have never been so frightened in my life.'

> The message came back that the leading troops were held up – couldn't get across the stream or across the bridge. Pop Pearson immediately stepped out to go forward. Last thing I said to him was: 'For God's sake, take care of yourself Pop', and, I can still remember the way he looked at me, he said: 'You take care of yourself, Harry'.
>
> Sadly he no sooner got to the bridge than he was shot by a sniper

from a tree, which was quickly avenged by Corporal Mackrell who, seeing the spot, riddled it with Sten gun fire and the German sniper's body fell out of the tree. I found out about that later of course. First thing I knew was that Desmond Keeling, the Intelligence officer who had gone forward with Pop and one of the company commanders, Bill Field, coming towards me saying: "Finito, there's no way forward".

Private Will Hanson remembers:

He heard we were making no progress; no more said, but he said he was going to go forward and we was to stop where we were. He jumped out of the carrier and away he went; and of course we did not see him again until...

Sergeant Jim Parkins was in 468 Battery of 94 Field Regiment, RA who were supporting 5 Wilts and recalled:

It was all on the wooded slopes we were firing at because they were being held up by machine guns and bangers, and all sorts. I don't think there were any SPs dug in on the side, but it was a hell of lot of machine guns.

Private Will Hanson, 5 Wiltshire.

Captain Peace had assumed command of the battalion:

I got on to Brigade and said that we would attempt a limited objective of the cross roads at la Varinière. And we did at least have a better idea where some of the enemy opposition was coming from so we were able to lay on a revised fire plan which, instead of the generalised barrage, was more likely to hit where we wanted it to hit.

With the only remaining company commander, Major Field, he inspired the men to fresh efforts. In the event, the barrage laid on in support of the attack outstripped the advance, but the tanks were still there and with them shooting up the road, the infantry pushed forward and beat the Germans down. Corporal Roy Cadogan in A Squadron 13th/18th:

...was behind Corporal Hennessey's tank; the infantry were supporting us either side – they were marching in single file on the road up to La Varinière. I remember seeing two or three of them just drop in the road and I thought: "They're dead!" I realised later of course that they were being fired on by some Germans who had dug in on the left hand side of the road on a sort of hummock; there was a machine gun post at the top which we subsequently destroyed.

Temporary graves outside the Regimental Aid Post of 5 Wiltshire, where Lieutenant Colonel Pearson was buried.

As the battle reached the houses near the objective, enemy started to come out with their hands up and over a hundred prisoners were taken between the bridge and la Varinière.

Sergeant Knowles went on the left with orders to clear the hedgerows and Bill Field went on the right. The meeting point would be the cross roads at la Varinière. I went down the middle of the road and, I don't know how it happened, but we captured La Varinière in twenty minutes. We hadn't got many chaps left, but we had more prisoners than we had men. I remember saying to the Sergeant Major: "Look, we can't afford two men to take these prisoners back, which you know are the instructions but if there is anybody who is a bit shaky send him back with the prisoners" to which he gave the splendid answer. "To tell you the truth, sir, they are all a bit shaky!" [Peace]

Just off the road they made these German prisoners dig graves. There were seven graves, if I remember rightly; they were taking quite a long time over it. It transpired that they thought they were going to be shot themselves and be put in the graves and they were digging graves for themselves. It wasn't so and one of the police corporals who took charge of them, after we had interrogated them, and took them back to Brigade

116

Headquarters or rear Battalion Headquarters, he let them know the holes weren't for them, but they were for those who had been killed, the Colonel, the Padre and others. [Garner]

By now the battalion strength was down to about seventy men and five officers.

I remember reporting to the brigade commander that we had got to la Varinière and he said: "Right, how do you feel about going on to Pinçon itself?" I said: "We'll get there alright" and I think I used an expression like, "We've got the bastards on the run" or something – one gets a bit stupid – "I don't know what the hell we'll do when we do get there because there aren't many of us left." Nonetheless he said: "Well, rightho, you go ahead."

At Battalion HQ, in a sunken track still littered with dead Germans, Captain Peace was giving out his orders when Major Milne, suddenly reappeared, running from the direction of the enemy. Soon after his capture an artillery salvo had come down and his captors:

... dived for cover. The enemy decided this was not a safe place to stay and withdrew. Major Milne pretended to be dead and was left behind. He was then able to rejoin and arrived, rather excitable and flourishing a German revolver he had picked up.

Just as we were ready to start a salvo came over and hit me. It was rather painful I seem to remember. I'd looked at chaps who'd been wounded and thought,' it doesn't seem to hurt very much, they didn't make much fuss'. Actually I felt as if someone had hit me with a bloody sledgehammer. Anyhow, I was quite vocal, or so I am told. They picked me up and put me on a stretcher, on the top of a jeep, took me back – and that was the end of my military career. [Peace]

Major Derrick Wormald:

I suppose it was at about 16.00 hrs that the final attack was launched on LA VARINIÈRE, with the Squadron giving maximum 'suppressive' fire, particularly on their left flank where we could see the enemy withdrawing.

Corporal Roy Cadogan

Having reached the village I suggested to our CO that another Squadron should be deployed on our Right flank, between the river and the village.

Captain Denny continued:

Lieutenant Elliot's troop . . . were not able to get off the road, as it was cut into the side of the hill, a sheer bank on one side and a steep drop on the other. Lieutenant Watt's troop followed and managed to find a way out to the right and took up a position there. ... The remainder of the Squadron were now over the river, and at this point in the proceedings five Boche infantry, all armed with bazookas, who had been sitting beside my tank on the road, came out of the hedge and gave themselves up, to my intense relief.

Another concentration was called for, on the village of la Varinière, and when this came down the attack went in with the sixty men and was successful. The squadron was now disposed to the east and north of the village and C Squadron came up on our right flank.'

Brigade HQ now ordered the battalion not to advance further, but to hold the crossroads. 4 Wiltshires were to be passed through to capture the hill itself.

British patrol during Operation BLUECOAT.

Chapter Ten

The Assault - Evening of 6 August

The weather was hot, the country damnable, and the Germans in the Mont Pinçon area even more bloody-minded than usual. Battle groups based on a couple of Tiger tanks were proving particularly noxious. I began to wonder how we would ever capture the formidable obstacle in front of us. As I drove back to my H.Q. on 6 August, I was met by a jubilant Pyman, who, even before we reached him, shouted out, 'We've got it! Mont Pinçon!' I could hardly believe my ears.

LIEUTENANT GENERAL SIR BRIAN HORROCKS

Cavalry Dash

When 129 Brigade Commander, Brigadier Mole, decided to pass 4 Wiltshire through their sister battalion to capture the hill, it was already 1800 hrs and the 4th were over two miles away on the left flank. The CO 13/18 Hussars, Vincent Dunkerly, was not prepared to wait and he ordered A Squadron to send a patrol to the top of the hill. By now Corporal Hennessey was on the far side of the stream:

At the base of the mountain, which seemed impossibly steep and covered with bushes and scrub. We milled around, dealing with pockets of enemy infantry in the undergrowth when, about 6 pm, we spotted a track which looked as if it may lead to the top, I reported this over the radio and was told to press on up it as fast as possible.

Captain Noel Denny:

150mm shells began bouncing on the cross-roads and in la Varinière itself. This pinned the infantry to the ground. Lieutenant Colonel VAB Dunkerly ... ordered Major Wormald to send an armoured patrol to the top of the hill, warning him at the same time that there were almost certainly 88mm anti-tank guns and enemy infantry in position on the summit. For the best part of two months the Regiment had been fighting in the closest possible co-operation with infantry, and it was considered a very dangerous performance in the close Normandy country to advance without infantry and artillery support. However, hope as ever springing eternal in the human heart, I set off with Lieutenant Elliot's and Lieutenant Jennison's troops to patrol to the top.

We advanced across a large wheat field, past a small wood on our right, which we shot up, but which did not, in fact, contain any enemy.

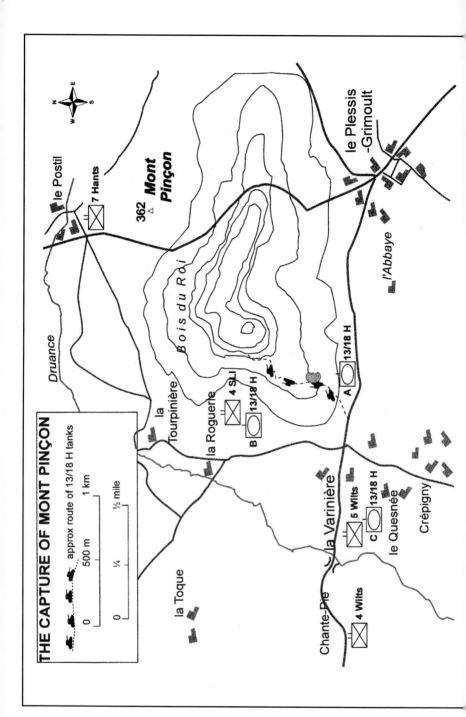

THE CAPTURE OF MONT PINÇON

approx route of 13/18 H tanks

0   500 m   1 km

0   ¼   ½ mile

le Postil

7 Hants

Druance

Bois du Roi

362 Mont Pinçon

le Plessis -Grimoult

l'Abbaye

la Tourpinière

la Roguerie

4 SLI

B 13/18 H

A 13/18 H

la Toque

la Varinière

5 Wilts

C 13/18 H

le Quesnée

Crépigny

Chante-Pie

4 Wilts

Then past some quarries, into one of which Corporal Davies's tank fell and overturned, and finally took up hull-down positions at the base of the hill proper, 2nd Troop right, 3rd Troop left.

Sergeant Rattle's tank (3rd Troop) then had its track blown off by an armour-piercing shot, but from which position it was impossible to tell. 2nd Troop and myself then laid a smoke screen, the first round of which, for once in a way, bounced absolutely right and blew very slowly in the right direction, completely blotting out the southern half of the position. ... During this movement we were not shot at once, the Boche being caught on the top looking east instead of west. By half-past six we had seven tanks in all-round position on the summit.

Pat Hennessey swung his tank round:

I was just about to head up this path when all of a sudden from my left another Sherman appeared and came racing across my bows with a friend of mine, a chap called Corporal Hammond leaning out of the turret, roaring with laughter and waving at me; and away he went up the track and I had to follow him. We both started racing up this track as if it was something of a game. I was furious with Hammond for going in front, in this piratical fashion, but away we went crashing up to the top. It was a hard run on a narrow track. There was a bank on the right as far as I can remember and a steep drop on the left. We went crashing up that with little or no opposition. Sergeant Rattle's tank, he was the troop sergeant, slithered into a quarry and very nearly overturned, but it didn't. Nevertheless we kept going. We could not stop to rescue him at that stage of the game because our orders were to get to the top as fast as possible. So he had to fall out of the procession.

The other seven managed to reach three quarters of the way up Mont Pinçon where we went into a holding position. We managed to do this by putting down a smoke screen that was highly successful and managed to cover up our rush to the top, which I think enabled us to have no casualties at all. [Elliot]

Noel Denny thought:

Contrary to expectations, it was much more pleasant at the top than at the bottom of Mont Pinçon, as it was a lovely summer evening. At 8 pm the Colonel came up and joined us, but there was still no sign of our infantry and we began to feel a trifle lonely. Shortly afterwards the remainder of the Squadron came up. As it was getting dark, we pulled into a very close leaguer.

The 13/18 Hussars were operating on a regimental net, ie all the wirelesses were tuned to the same frequency, as opposed to each squadron having its own frequency. This was preferable for

'*Capture of Mont Pinçon*' from a painting by Donald Hunt (Troop leader 13/18 Hussars in 1944).

those occasions when the whole regiment was engaged in the same operation as it meant that everyone could hear what was going on. However, it required a high standard of wireless discipline. In B Squadron, Hugh Franks:

> *Suddenly, I heard this voice coming up on the wireless and it was Noel Denny and he said, in a very loud voice, "It is a lovely summer evening, there don't seem to be any other people up here, but I feel very lonely".*

While in Regimental Headquarters they were:

> *...trying to relate the progress of this back to Brigade and all the other people who seemed to be extremely concerned and interested in what was going on!* [Neave]

The 'lovely summer evening' was soon obscured by thick mist and Corporal Hennessey:

> *...we couldn't see very far but we could hear German voices*

shouting. Having got to the top of the mountain we were told to stay there. In fact there was nowhere else to go, so we did and we had to wait there for some hours, I suppose. It was very lonely and a bit eerie, in that we couldn't see very far. When we heard the Germans we put a shot across where we could hear their sound and that really is how we spent the next couple of hours waiting for the infantry to arrive.

A Squadron Leader, Derrick Wormald was having problems:

After we had taken up positions to the east and north of the village [la Varinière] it was heavily 'stonked' by enemy medium artillery, during which time I decided to move my tank. There was a large explosion and it came to a shuddering halt. I thought that we had been hit by a medium shell. After the 'stonking' ended I dismounted to inspect the damage. As I jumped from the hull I noticed that I was descending with my feet about to land on a German Teller (tank) mine. I separated my feet and landed astride it. . . I radioed for the squadron's ARV [armoured recovery vehicle] to come to my assistance, which it did, but not before it was engaged by enemy anti tank weapons from our right flank as it crossed the cross-roads in the village. We attached a tow rope to my tank and commenced a tow. There was another explosion. The ARV had also run over a mine and become immobile. Unfortunately two crew members were sitting on the front of my tank at the time and they were wounded by the displacement of track plates which we had welded to the front hull of our tanks to give extra frontal armour, particularly against panzerfausts (an early form of spaced armour).

While Major Wormald was helping to bandage up his casualties, Regimental Headquarters arrived:

I climbed up on the Commanding Officer's tank. He told me to get moving to join the other two troops of my Squadron on the summit of the hill. My hands were dripping casualty blood and I explained that I had a mobility problem at that moment. He was not impressed. However, as soon as possible, I hitch-hiked/commandeered a lift to the summit on another of my Squadron's tanks. A replacement was not long in arriving – because I always encouraged the Squadron Fitters ... to hold and travel in one or two spare tanks. During the day we were fortunate that the enemy had not deployed anti tank guns or tanks against us. Presumably they considered that the terrain was tank proof and that it could be held by infantry with bazookas; with which our suppressive fire could deal, whilst we were on the move. Also 7 Armoured Division had been trying to capture the hill from the north for some time and in addition major attacks were being launched further *to the east. Therefore their armour was already committed elsewhere and we had found a soft spot in their defences.*

Once the infantry had arrived, possibly about twenty minutes later than that, two more tanks came up and joined us followed by the rest of A Squadron, which also deployed across the feature of Mont Pinçon, in conjunction with the infantry Vincent Dunkerly literally came up within fifty yards of where we were. [Elliot]

In A Squadron Fitters Troop, Trooper Douglas Wileman:

I was taking wireless watch for the two vehicles when 13B, the ARV, was called up to see to Major Wormald's tank which was in trouble, blown the track, or some problem and the ARV went up to carry out the recovery.

**Trooper Douglas Wileman,
13th/18th Royal Hussars**

4th Somerset Light Infantry and B Squadron

Over on the left flank, the CO 4 Som LI, Lieutenant Colonel ('Lippy') Lipscomb, could see the tanks on top of the hill and quickly resumed his advance, this time with a troop from B Squadron which had managed to reach him. One tank managed to negotiate minefield, hedges and stream and got into a position from which it could blast the hillside. 'This action by one tank proved the turning-point of the battle. .'

Lieutenant Hugh Franks was the troop leader:

I was beginning to hear quite a lot of machine gun fire ahead of me which I reported to 'Dag' [Rugge-Price] – my squadron leader. I went forward and saw a group of infantrymen, lying flat on the ground or crouching behind trees or taking cover wherever they could. I had a bit of luck then because I remember seeing suddenly fire coming from one of the Spandau machine guns which were holding up the infantry. I was able to send a few HE shells that way and also to fire the Browning machine gun from the turret and that silenced them.

Captain Bobby Neave, the squadron second-in-command:

. . . B Squadron were told to go round to the north side of Mont Pinçon. There were a lot of roads running out of the north west corner of it, which was defended by rather intelligent light troops, who had one

*or two craftily dug in anti tank guns, so that we had to watch out; I was given the task of knocking out two of them and I with, I think, two other tanks had been detached by Dag to go round to the north to do this task.
... we were going to expose ourselves, so I laid a smoke screen; I think we succeeded either in knocking them out or making them go off the hill.
... by evening, say 9 o'clock, the SLI and I had cleared our area and they went on up the mountain side.*

130 Brigade
Further to the left, preparation had continued for the renewed attack by 7 Hants on Roucamps. In view of the progress which had now been made on 129 Brigade's front that could be cancelled and HQ 130 Brigade withdrew the Hampshires to a defensive position round Plecière. They had advanced to the foot of Mount Pinçon and had successfully achieved the desired distraction from 129 Brigade's attack.

Lieutenant Hugh Franks, 13th/18th Royal Hussars

Climbing Mont Pinçon
As dusk fell, C and D Companies of 4 Som LI advanced in single file through A and B Companies, with a view to infiltrating the enemy position. Sydney Jary recalled:

A cold and damp mist descended which, with the fading light, gave us welcome cover but also wretched discomfort. We were still in shirtsleeves, which became damp from the sweat of our exertion climbing the steep lower slopes. Alert, with pistol in hand, I anticipated a sudden brush with an enemy post. Not a shot was fired. By some miracle we passed right through their positions without being detected. Our luck had changed.

Up the hill we scrambled, through the trees, until we reached the rocky gorse-covered summit. Through the mist German voices could be heard calling to each other, unaware that, by stealth, we were now king of the castle.

Throughout the day we had experienced trouble with our 18 Set radios and, consequently, it proved impossible to inform Lippy of our success. Gordon Bennetts, our Battalion Intelligence Officer, managed to reach us but he too was cut off and could get no messages to Lippy. It was finally decided that one of my Platoon should try to slip back through the German positions. I chose Sergeant Kingston but suggested that it was really a job for two, so Private Bull went too. Jim Kingston was briefed by Gordon and a message for Lippy was concealed in the epaulette of his shirt.

...Bearing in mind that the whole Company had infiltrated the enemy positions, it seemed likely that, by now, our penetration had been discovered and the opposition would be alert. I was wrong. Hidden by both night and mist, Jim Kingston successfully reached Battalion Headquarters, although he had to leave Private Bull, who had fallen and injured his knee, with the 4th Wiltshires.

It is incredible when you look back. Those German machine guns had stopped us absolutely dead. We couldn't move forward backward or sideways. You would think they would have heard us coming but we followed a track up the hill chiefly because, if you are walking through a wooded area in the dark you do not have the control of your platoon, but you do if you are on a track. At the least sign of trouble you'd scatter to each side. Marching up the hill – I say marching but walking up the hill – we could hear voices coming out of the mist, German voices, but we didn't meet a soul...

When Corporal Proctor got to the top:

...Mr Jary gave us orders to dig in. It's easy giving an order but complying with the order is a different matter! We dug about six inches deep and then we hit solid rock. We only had small trenching tools so we put the spoil to the side of the trenches to give ourselves as much protection as we could. Meanwhile we were still in shirtsleeves, cold and shivering. All we wanted was something to eat and to drink.

Captain Denny in A Squadron, on the summit:

. . . the 4th Somerset Light Infantry began to arrive and dig in around us. Their intelligence officer talked to some Boches who could clearly be heard digging in less than one hundred yards from us, oblivious of our presence. They were made aware of it by a 75mm shell which went just above their breakfast table next morning.

B Squadron 13/18 Hussars were also trying to get to the summit:

'Dag' Rugge-Price must have got a compass bearing on to the top of the hill from the people who were already up there because he came across to me and said: "Hugh, what I'm going to do, I'm going to walk in front of your tank with a compass." I said: "Oh, isn't that a bit risky? There might still be a lot of Boches around on the way up". And he said, "No, I don't think there are. I've got the bearing which should bring us up somewhere near where the tanks are at the top." So I said, "OK, what about the interference to the compass from the metal of our tank?" He said "I've thought of that I'll keep about fifteen, twenty yards ahead of

you." I thought it was a very brave thing for him to have done.

4 Wiltshire

4 Wilts under Lieutenant Colonel Ted Luce had now reached la Varinière, where what remained of 5 Wilts were holding out against continued counter-attacks from le Quesnée. At about 2100 hrs B Company led the exhausted battalion up the hill, passing dead comrades from the 5th Battalion on the way. After the savage battle at St Jean-le-Blanc, they had had to march seven miles to the reserve area at Danvou, only to come under punishing shellfire. Now they had marched forward from following up 4 Som LI on the left flank. They moved in single file through 'bewildered Germans who were still clinging to positions on the slope'. One of the company commanders, Major Parsons, described the trek:

> Enemy resistance was slight and the chief difficulty was the physical effort of climbing, for the slope soon became very steep and covered with scrub. It was a strange feeling, as we toiled up, heavily laden with weapons ammunition, picks and shovels, expecting to find ourselves surrounded at any moment. The sergeant, commanding the leading platoon, very resourcefully told his men that they were not doing an attack, but were going up to relieve another unit already there. This materially helped the speed of the advance.
>
> As we neared the top a thick fog came down. We could see no landmarks but we found the tanks. They were relieved to see us, for Germans could be heard shouting and digging in close by. We were as tired as any troops could be, and many of us fell asleep as we were digging positions in the rocky soil, falling headlong pick in hand into the half-dug trenches, 'dead to the wide'.

Corporal Douglas Proctor, 4 Somerset Light Infantry.

Lieutenant Colonel Luce told Harry Peace later that:

> When the brigadier told him to go and get to Mont Pinçon any way he liked, but suggested a certain route, he gave the classic answer, 'Thank you very much, I'll go where my friends are.' This meant a very long and exhausting march for them to come round to our position, but I think it probably demonstrates the trust the two battalions had developed in each other. He reckoned that where we'd made the break

was the place for him to reinforce.

At one stage, the battalion was held up:

> *Colonel Luce realised we were held up, the whole battalion was held up, something drastic had to be done, and he took over as the leading man of the leading section and you can imagine the morale of the battalion with your commanding officer having the courage to do that! And he led the way up. Then half way up he was suddenly confronted with a couple of chaps, Germans, with a machine gun. In fluent German, which consisted of shouting English in a very loud voice he told them to surrender – which they did.* [Powell]

And they were a welcome sight to the lonely tank crews on the summit:

> *The infantry were extremely tired. The 4th Wilts as well as what was left of the 5th had been under extreme pressure for nearly two days, non-stop, and they were extremely hungry. So, as usual, our Regiment fed them; we always had plenty of compo packs and plenty of spare food aboard. And they were always first thing given hot cups of tea from our pressure cookers – which perked their morale up considerably.* [Elliot]

In the Commanding Officer's tank, Julius Neave looked back at 6 August:

> *A busy day. Our intention is to capture Mont Pinçon – the biggest feature in Normandy – with a very depleted infantry brigade and tired armoured regiment. It is undoubtedly a most important objective – but again a Boy doing a Man's job.*
>
> *Went off to the 129 Brigade 'O' Group after a very unpleasant breakfast stonk, when the Brigadier gave out excellent orders and gave us till 1400 hrs to get the battle tee-ed up.*
>
> *A large barrage started the thing off and very little progress was made at all, in fact we gazed at the bloody mountain with no hope at all. However they started again and off went the Boche – this was on the right and A Squadron pushed into the village of Varinière while the right remained pretty static.*
>
> *It was at this stage that higher command took a hand and started bogging things up left, right and centre. Instead of telling us to carry on, they frigged about for hours despite the Colonel's very clear information to them after we had been up to the village to have a look-see. Eventually we sent off two patrols, one onto the top of the mountain and one along the south slope to watch "Bloody Village" or Plessis Grimoult. The patrol got onto the ridge without much trouble and sat there only being stonked and after quite a lot of Boche had given themselves up. The right-hand troop got hopelessly bogged and*

la
Tourpinière

a Roguerie

△ 362

l'Abbaye

le Plessis
-Grimoult

Mont Pinçon – montage of aerial photographs by 2nd Tactical Air Force 24
June 1944. The dotted circle shows the area where the Germans had
installed a radio navigation aid for their aircraft and which had clearly been
the target of Allied bombers – as can be seen by the bomb craters. © Crown
Copyright/MOD

surrounded by Boche but managed to keep them off.

We were screaming all the time on the blower that the higher command simply had to make up their minds. The Colonel said that he was either going to take the Squadron off the mountain or take the whole Regiment up or they had to put some infantry on it too, and also that they must look after his communications, where C Squadron were sitting with a very battered battalion, they were literally almost surrounded by not really very hostile Boche – but ones not yet in a surrendering mood.

Eventually when nothing more came from Brigade the Colonel decided to get onto the top with A and B and RHQ. . . taking a very doubtful route where bazooka men were reported in the failing light. However, we made it eventually and I was heartily thankful to find myself on top of the mountain . . . What had looked a great height from down below was a terrific sight on top and the view wonderful until the mist came down and visibility was about five feet. This made it quite impossible for the column behind us after they had been delayed by the self-propelled guns who were blocking the road behind the village.

We had a quiet night – thank God! but heard in the morning that the Boche had mounted a counter attack to drive us off, consisting of 6 Panthers, 6 self-propelled guns and some infantry. By great luck they lost their way in the mist, ran into our shelling and gave up!

Chapter Eleven

Elsewhere on 5 and 6 August

7 Armoured Division entered Aunay-sur-Odon during the afternoon and forward troops pushed on about four miles in the direction of Thury Harcourt. ...

As American troops advanced on Vire from the south-west, tanks of 11 Armoured Division were fighting north of the town. In the 8 Corps sector most of 5 August was spent mopping up the enemy pockets which were hindering the supply routes. ...Throughout 6 August the enemy was attacking between Vire and Mont Pinçon. 10 SS Panzer Division made a determined attack against 11 Armoured Division and achieved some initial success, but the ground lost was quickly retaken.

NORMANDY TO THE BALTIC

XXX Corps
Aunay-sur-Odon and Villers-Bocage
7th Armoured Division

To the north of 43rd Division, the streets of both Villers-Bocage and Aunay were so badly blocked that, although tanks and infantry of 7th Armoured Division could get through, neither town would be feasible for the divisional centre line until the engineers and pioneers had cleared routes through. It was difficult to see where the streets had been in the shambles of bombed buildings and cratered roads. Aunay was even worse than Villers-Bocage, with only the shells of the church and one other building standing. The division's Medical War Diary described the areas round Aunay as 'full of dead and decomposing cattle and Germans-mines and booby traps very plentiful'. 209 Field Company, Royal Engineers, of XXX Corps Troops Engineers, had to use bulldozers to create routes. In the first twenty-four hours the company cleared 1,500 yards of street, and created some 2,000 yards of diversion routes.

However, during 5 August, 22 Armoured Brigade's swing to the left north of Aunay had taken them sixteen miles, beyond Bonnemaison, before they encountered enemy defences on the high ground north of Hamars. The whole division was therefore diverted on to the road running south through la Vallée heading

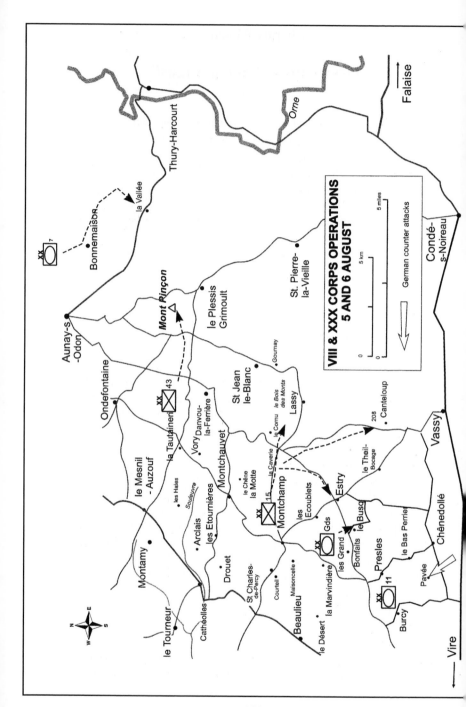

VIII & XXX CORPS OPERATIONS
5 AND 6 AUGUST

German counter attacks

0   5 km
0   5 miles

east of Mont Pinçon. After dark 7 Queen's pushed on to tackle la Vallée and, just before midnight, their leading company was in the village - which was densely mined. By 0330 hrs next day the battalion had cleared it of enemy and with the sappers set about clearing the mines in the darkness. Throughout the 6th the whole area was came under attack from enemy artillery and mortars.

They were now on a fairly open plateau north-east of, and overlooked by, Mont Pinçon. But between them and Mount Pinçon was a deep wooded – and heavily mined – valley. The Queen's and the Divisional Engineers spent the night of the 6th and much of the 7th August tackling the minefields, under frequent shellfire.

Further west, 6 Queen's were involved in sharp fighting, by the end of which the battalion strength had been reduced to that of a company.

50th Division

50th Division had been relieved on 5 August and moved out of the front-line for a few days – their first break since landing on D-Day.

VIII Corps

The Vire-Estry Line
15th Division

The plan for 5 August was for the division to break through the Germans at la Caverie in the direction of Lassy, one of VIII Corps' original BLUECOAT objectives. 227 Brigade, who were to pass through 44 Brigade, were carried forward on the Scots Guards' tanks from the southern slopes of Quarry Hill. By midday the three battalions were through Montchauvet and continued their advance eastward, the Argylls along the Montchamp-la Caverie road, the HLI and the Gordons towards 'Au Cornu'. ['Au Cornu' was presumably la Chapelle au Cornu, north-west of le Cornu?] By the time that the Argylls halted for the night, they were covering the bridge about a mile short of la Caverie and had made no contact with the enemy. However, when the HLI reached 'Au Cornu', they suffered a number of casualties from heavy shelling and the Gordons were shelled round the crossroads south of it.

Two operations were planned for the next day. From la

Caverie crossroads 227 Brigade was to establish a firm base in and around Estry, while 46 Brigade attacked eastward to cover the northern flank towards Mount Pinçon.

In 6 Guards Tank Brigade, when orders were issued for an advance by the whole brigade on 6 August, some thought that a recent statement of the German High Command to the effect that 'the whole front in Normandy has been engulfed by the British and American offensive' offered prospects of a rapid advance instead of inch by inch progress. They were to be disillusioned.

46 Brigade opened the day's operations, advancing south-

British infantry moving towards Mont Pinçon under a scorching August sun. Note the corporal is carring Bren gun magazines in his ammunition pouch. The Bren gunner is behind him.

east to the steep hill, le Bois des Monts. Across a valley two hundred feet below was Gournay. The Germans held the slopes and Gournay itself in strength and 46 Brigade met heavy artillery and machine-gun fire. Tanks could not get off the road, which was covered by shellfire and blocked by burning vehicles. Three companies of Cameronians were pinned by fire in the valley bottom and their Battalion Headquarters suffered particularly severely. 'For the Cameronians this was indeed "Black Sunday."'

Under heavy mortar-fire the Glasgow Highlanders had now taken up position in the Bois des Monts and the Seaforth, with a squadron of the Coldstream, were intended to pass through them and occupy Lassy. They anticipated not meeting any enemy short of Lassy but at about 1500 hrs the leading company ran into heavy fire as they went over the crest of the hill leading down into the valley. Although they wiped out the nearer of the German outposts, the company was pinned down on the forward slopes and was soon reduced to about forty men and one officer. The Seaforth's new Commanding Officer, Lieutenant Colonel Robertson, was mortally wounded and the Coldstream squadron had a number of their tanks knocked out by well-concealed 88s.

A battalion attack with two fresh companies could get only about a hundred and fifty yards forward – at the cost of heavy casualties from intense artillery and small-arms fire, including both company commanders. The advance in that direction had to be abandoned.

Meanwhile 227 Brigade farther south-west also met tough resistance. Their objectives were the crossroads on the ridge at Estry, Hill 208 overlooking Canteloup and the ridge at le Theil-Bocage. It soon became clear that,

> 9th S.S. Panzer Division had turned Estry into a strong-point, which it meant to hold at all costs. Two or three companies of an SS regiment, a dug-in tank, 88-mm guns, bazookas, mortars, Nebelwerfers, machine-gun nests, mines-all were there, and the garrison had a call on powerful artillery farther back.

The action had begun when the Gordons ran into a minefield half a mile from the Estry crossroads. Their leading company reached the crossroads, but could get no farther. Another company tried another route, but was stopped short of the village after losing four of the supporting tanks. Neither of the

135

remaining companies each accompanied by two SP guns was successful in attempts to turn the village on either flank. 'In the maze of walls and lanes and ditches there was little room to manoeuvre, and the field of fire was seldom as much as fifty yards.'

The Gordons dug in on the eastern outskirts of Estry and, after a medium artillery barrage, the HLI and Scots Guards attacked through them. Despite some progress the resistance they met caused heavy casualties and as darkness closed in, they were forced to withdraw and dig in beside the Scots Guards tanks in close leaguer. 'Hardly were the HLI dug in when the enemy swept the orchards with a heavy concentration of medium artillery.'

By evening the Argylls, with their supporting squadron of Scots Guards, had taken most of the near side of Hill 208, but mines, heavy machine-gun and mortar-fire halted them some three hundred yards short of the main enemy positions on the crest. Dug-in tanks and SP 88mm guns had also caused them a lot of trouble. They were forced to dig in for the night on the slopes.

Although 3 Irish Guards occupied les Ecoublets without opposition on 7 August, 15th Division was confronted with a determined defence at Estry and suffered severe casualties getting into the northern outskirts after. The Germans were clearly not going to let the Vire-Estry line go without a bitter struggle – the Mortain counter-attack was to be made that day. General O'Connor therefore decided that the two armoured divisions should hold the line in the centre of the Corps' front, while infantry exerted pressure on either side.

Guards Armoured Division

After the capture of Maisoncelles and Montchamp the Grenadier Group had found nothing between St Charles-de-Percy and la Marvindière except for the burnt-out shells of destroyed German tanks. That had raised hopes that the Germans might be preparing to withdraw from le Busq and Estry and 5 Coldstream, with 2 Irish Guards, were told to seize le Busq. Irish Guards were then to clear the road up to Estry so that 15th Division could make an attack on the 7th.

The Coldstream group's move on le Busq began at 1600 hrs on 6 August, but after reaching the road on the summit without

A burnt out Panzer MkIV.

major problems they ran into fire on the far side. The leading companies and tanks suffered heavy casualties before they were drawn back to the near side of the ridge – which effectively denied the far side to the enemy.

11th Armoured Division

General Roberts wrote: 'There is no doubt we remained in highly precarious situation for several days.' He had sent a message to all troops:

I wish all ranks to know that during the present period of operation, tremendous demands will be made on their powers of endurance. I will only call upon troops to do the almost impossible but not the completely impossible. The stakes are high and the prize great.

During 5 August, 9th SS Panzer Division attacked 3 Monmouthshires and 2 Fife and Forfarshire in their Pavée 'box', but were driven off by the defenders and 'massive Corps artillery defensive fire programmes'. But it was not until 1800 hrs on 6 August that the major onslaught came onto a salient described by a German general as 'a festering abscess'. It was by 10th SS Panzer Division augmented by various units, including a tank battalion from 110th Panzer Division, a battalion of engineers fighting as infantry, tanks and SP guns from the Heavy Tank battalion of II SS Panzer Corps – as well as most of the newly arrived 363rd Division. The attack started as 185 Brigade from 3rd Division was about to take over in the centre, so 29 Armoured Brigade with 2 Warwicks held to the left of them and 159 Brigade plus 1 Norfolks on the right.

The fierce battle went on into the night, with the VIII Corps artillery firing almost non-stop. General Roberts thought:

> *It was certainly the toughest battle we had in the campaign: both sides received heavy casualties but the Germans had the heavier largely because they were advancing and not dug in. If it had not been for the Corps artillery, I doubt if we would have held the Germans.*

Chapter Twelve

Night on Mont Pinçon and in la Varinière
(6/7 August)

43 Division finally secured Mount Pinçon and some villages on the southern slopes, but heavy fighting continued and the enemy launched repeated counter attacks in which considerable casualties were inflicted by both sides. Normandy to the Baltic

La Varinière

The much-depleted 5 Wiltshire had been left with C Squadron 13/18 Hussars, under Major Sir Delaval Cotter, to hold the village and crossroads of la Varinière. It was vital that the they should be held, otherwise withdrawal from Mont Pinçon would be inevitable Their capture had cost 5 Wiltshire fifty-two killed and 158 wounded and they were still not cleared of enemy; there were a number still in the surrounding woods and orchards. A new Commanding Officer, Lieutenant Colonel Bill Roberts from 4 Somerset Light Infantry, had taken over 5 Wiltshire during the evening with Captain Keeling, the Intelligence Officer, as his Adjutant.

In order to prepare the strongest possible defence around la Varinière the small number of men were formed into a tight circle around the crossroads, with tanks positioned to thicken up the defence as well as guard against counter-attack. A Company under Major Milne:

> ...*stayed put around the cross-roads till the following night and in those twenty-four hours all the muck in the world came down on us, but considering everything we didn't get too many further casualties. I held the north of the cross-roads and in the morning they put in a counter attack and against me and things got to the grenade throwing stage, but we finally saw them off.*

And 94 Field Regiment, where David Hadow was a Forward Observation

Captain David Hadow, 94 Field Regiment RA.

139

Officer, played a major part in seeing them off:

> Bill Roberts and the battery commander, Ted Lequesne sat there all night looking at their map and picking targets which would be profitable to engage, places where they thought the enemy might be forming up or where they would have to pass through in order to get to a forming up point. We know from prisoners that some of those targets were very successful and appropriate.
>
> The guns were always loaded and laid on to a pre-agreed target, an "SOS" line, at night and fired as soon as we had the request for fire. It might have been a machine gun nest, a mortar site or a spot from where an attack might be launched. [Parkins]

Later, when one counter-attack developed:

> . . . fortunately there was a lot of mist and according to a PW they became rather lost and halted on the road just south of us, and were caught by one of Queenie's [Major Ted Lequesne]'stonks'... This broke them up completely, but a few patrols got through and we had enemy within a hundred yards of Battalion HQ most of the night.

During the afternoon of the 6th, C Squadron 13/18 Hussars had been supporting A Squadron, by watching their south and south-western flanks. When the A Squadron troops were ordered up the hill, a troop from C was sent to reconnoitre between la Varinière and le Plessis Grimoult.

> Owing to the boggy nature of the ground near LA VARINIERE all 1st Troop became bogged and 2nd Troop were sent out to help them; they managed to recover two of these tanks but the remaining two had to be left as they were in enemy country. One of these two tanks were hit and Tprs. Challis and Haskayne were killed, the remainder of the crews together with 2/Lt. Edwards eventually regained our lines on foot later that night. The dismounted crews were returned to the Echelon, but on their way back were ambushed. – Tpr. Wallace being killed, Cpl Roden and Tpr Whent wounded.

At about 2100 hrs Brian Edwards was told by Delaval Cotter to:

> Take my troop down the road towards Le Plessis Grimoult, round the south side of Mont Pinçon, to find out if there were any German troops in that area. We turned off the road when the land to the right opened up. We left the road and started to travel across the first of these fields. At first the ground seemed quite hard no problem but after we had gone a short way it was clear that we had got in a bog at the end of the field. Two tanks including mine became bogged down. Some time later Delaval Cotter sent Roddy Norris, who was second in command of the Squadron, over to us in the field and he decided that the tanks were too

The *Panzerjäger* made its first appearance in Normandy in June 1944. It had an 88mm gun on a Panther chassis.

heavily bogged down to move them and that we would return. Before that happened, while we were still on the ground and not in the tanks, the Germans behind the hedge engaged us with a panzerfaust knocking out both tanks and as the crews they tried to escape through the turret they were cut down by machine gun fire.

In leaguer for the night the remainder of the squadron found it unexpectedly quiet. Delaval Cotter:

...realised the Germans were likely to infiltrate on foot, so we dismounted somebody from each tank, with a machine gun, to keep watch. I think I was more concerned that Haygarth, my troop sergeant, and my tanks were the only tanks that could line up against this German 88 mm SP. Both of our guns were lined up on it as it lay in wait

and we sat all night long wondering when he was going to appear. He
eventually came out as soon as he could see at first light and Sergeant
Haygarth was ready and drilled him through straight away.

With daylight C Squadron took up a defensive position near le Quesnée and a troop was sent to clear the outskirts of the village. 'The enemy flew white flags but would not come out to surrender.'

The most determined attack on A Company came through the early morning mist. Their defences had had to be sited in a number of kitchen gardens criss-crossed by hedges and ditches, which made the company's field of fire very limited. The enemy had formed up in a house to the south of the position and, with the ample cover, were able to crawl undetected to within a few yards of the Wiltshiremen. A violent battle then began with grenades and small arms fire, but eventually the enemy were beaten back. They left behind many dead and now apparently had had enough, as they did not attempt another counter-attack. Nevertheless shelling and mortaring of both the Wiltshire positions and their line of communication continued.

As well as the 88mm SP destroyed by C Squadron, a number of enemy infantry were killed or taken while the small garrison held on for the twenty-four hours needed for Mont Pinçon to be reinforced

Overnight Moves

At midnight on the 6th, General Thomas ordered 214 Brigade to move forward as fast as possible and clear the Mont Pinçon feature up to the main road from Aunay-sur-Odon. 7 Armoured Division, after many setbacks, was at last moving that way in order to thrust due south on Condé-sur-Noireau. This made the capture of the road centre at le Plessis Grimoult especially urgent and that task was also given to 214 Brigade. 130 Brigade was to continue its advance towards Roucamps, on the main road north of Mont Pinçon.

Sharing Mont Pinçon with the Enemy

Julius Neave recalls:

Although we were quite unaware of this and we knew the Germans
were not very far away and people had heard the Germans talking at the
top, a counter attack was mounted by them to push us off the top. But
they lost their way in the fog, which came down pretty heavily and

stayed right until dawn next morning. It wasn't until first light next morning that the shelling began again because I don't think they'd got themselves sorted out and then I remember a very hairy morning when we were shelled all the time. Remarkably we had very comparatively few casualties.

He had written in his diary for 7 August:

At first light Sim [Earl of Feversham, Second-in-Command] and party with Dag [Rugge-Price] and Derrick [Wormald] joined us and the mist cleared early – at about the same time the shelling started and they obviously meant to give it to us hot because it went on without stopping almost all the morning and until we were relieved by the 4th/7th at midday.

Dag went off about 0700 hrs to capture the eastern ring contour and got it OK pushing off the top some rather dejected Boche. The Som LI came through about 1000 hrs and joined them; altogether things looked good except for enemy infiltrations along our communications, which we had anticipated and reported without anything being done! However the KRRC and 4th/7th were well on their way and prevented anything like that happening ...

At 0530 hrs B Squadron had moved out to 'the 360 contour' and were later followed by 4 Som LI. They then moved further forward to a position to cover le Plessis Grimoult and engage SP guns and mortars which had been giving them trouble were engaged: 'Heavy shelling and mortaring continued from first light and two ARVs were hit.'

At the same time A Squadron moved into defensive positions with 4 Wilts at the western end of the crest. Douglas Wileman in A Squadron Fitters' Troop:

Then there was C Squadron's ARV – the next thing we heard was that C Squadron ARV had been hit and there were casualties on it. We didn't hear anything more until Captain McMichael, the Tech Adj came in to where we were and said, 'Sorry to tell you, you haven't got an ARV. C Squadron and A Squadron ARVs have both been destroyed. There are fatal casualties, I can't tell you yet exactly who was killed or what's happened.'

At least one German patrol had reached the 4 Wilts' positions during the night. When first light came next morning 'Dim' Robbins found:

To my dismay – horror – a German patrol had got into my company lines undetected and had captured my two signallers who were in the, so-called, trench next to me, five yards away. I got up in the morning

143

and shouted across to the signallers: 'Contact Battalion HQ'; no reply;
I went over to see if they were asleep, but there was nothing there but
their sets. We never saw or heard of those two signallers again – even
after the War.

214 Brigade

Following the orders for 214 Brigade to clear Mont Pinçon, the reconnaissance groups of 1 Worcestershire and 7 Somerset Light Infantry, at once set off. They reached the crest through the mist soon after first light while the seconds-in-command were bringing the battalions forward. As the sun burnt out the mist, 'every gun and mortar the enemy could muster opened up; around la Varinière crossroads the shelling by 88's became particularly intense, continuous and accurate.' The routes from la Varinière up Mont Pinçon were covered by direct enemy fire and the two battalions had to move up the hill under heavy shelling and mortaring. But, by the middle of the morning, the 7th had relieved 4 Somerset Light Infantry on the crest. 1 Worcestershire followed and by 1130 had taken over from 4 Wiltshire at the western end and two squadrons 4/7 Dragoon Guards took over from the 13th/18th squadrons. The latter escorted 4 Wilts and 4 Som LI back and concentrated in the area of Danvou.

> *Eventually we were relieved the next day. I suppose we had some*
> *breakfast – I don't really remember. As we were coming down the hill*
> *towards the cross roads at the bottom of the hill we found HQ Company and*
> *the cooks had been shelled.* [Trim]

The 13th/18th:

> *Had extra smart stonk just before pulling out and a very super one*
> *on arrival at our rally which was most unkind and very unpleasant. We*
> *filled up and pushed on to le Mesnil Auzouf to harbour and before we*
> *got there C Squadron was released and started to join us.*

C Squadron had had to remain until 1700 when 5 DCLI relieved 5 Wilts. Before that they were still dealing with enemy infantry who had been infiltrating and 'causing a certain amount of concern in the Gun areas'.

130 Brigade

7 Hants had been given the task for 7 August of clearing the area round Roucamps and Pasty. After that they took over the defence of the reverse slopes of Mount Pinçon, 'to be held at all

costs'. Company Sergeant Major of D Company, Laurie Symes, was in Company Headquarters when:

> Some French ladies came in. Apparently there were a number of elderly French men and children in the open away to our right flank. They had no food and were very frightened. The Company Commander told me to take my carrier over to them. I went with some compo and the French ladies – and the company runner – about half a mile away over open grassland, down a steep slope with some woods and there in a fold in the ground was a collection of French people – and four or five horses. We off-loaded the compo packs and while we were doing it five or so mortar bombs came down on the edge of the fold. There were no casualties to people, but legs of two of the horses were broken. I shot them with a Sten gun. With hindsight it amazes me; the Germans must have known who they were firing at, but were going to have a go at two British soldiers and a carrier.

> The countryside was one big stink; it was a commonplace to see bloated cows, horses, upside down, legs in the air – caught in the open by shellfire. It was very upsetting but you eventually got used to it. The air seemed permanently full of dust and the smell of cordite. Then there was the noise of AP going through tanks, the occasional scream of a man who had been wounded, a burst of machine gun fire.

The Abbey

During the battle the inhabitants of the villages and hamlets round Mont Pinçon tried to find safety as best they could. For

The abbey 1939.

The abbey 1944.

some of those that remained the abbey, between la Varinière and le Plessis Grimoult, provided an uneasy place of refuge. The present owner is M. Le Marchand:

The Abbey has existed since the 12th Century; it seems to have been able to resist time itself. It has also resisted the various conflicts of The Hundred Years' War. As a result there is a feeling of solidity, endurance and also permanence. Hence the idea of a place of refuge... The Germans installed an anti-aircraft gun, a rapid firing gun The British spotted the gun and tried to put it out of action. They bombarded the Abbey. The Germans made a hole in the vault to gain access to the top of the tower which they used as a forward observation post from which to direct their artillery.

Mme Jeanne Groult:

I was 17 years old; we had not evacuated. That was a mistake because we were being fired on by artillery. There was a gun next to our shelter which had been spotted by the British. The Abbey was next door to us and the firing was intense and when we left it was unbearable.

Trooper George Treloar of 13/18 Hussars:

The abbey 2002.

VOUS QUI   SOUVENEZ-

L'AVEZ   VOUS

CONNU   DANS

ET AIME   VOS PRIÈRES

de

André Daniel VAUCLAIR

tué sous le feu d'artillerie au Plessis-Grimoult

le 8 Août 1944

dans sa 16ᵉ année.

Je meurs mais mon amour ne meurt pas, je vous aimerai dans le ciel comme je vous ai aimés sur la terre.   *(B. Berchmans.)*

Consolez vous avec moi vous tous qui m'êtes si chers, car dans l'âge où tout sourit j'abandonne cette vallée de larmes c'est pour le royaume des cieux.

Je croyais voir le lendemain, Seigneur, et vous avez tranché mes jours entre un soir et un matin.

                                   (Isaïe.)

Seigneur, vous nous avez emporté comme un tourbillon celui qui nous était si cher et qui faisait la joie et le bonheur de notre vie.

Ceux qui le virent en passant le regrettent, ceux qui le connurent le pleurent. Les siens qui l'aimaient le regrettent et le pleureront toujours.

Miséricordieux Jésus, donnez-lui le repos éternel

R. Poulain, phot. Flers (Orne)

Memorial to André Vauclair: 'wounded at 9 o'clock in the morning and died at 4 o'clock that afternoon.'

**Trooper George Treloar
13th/18th Royal Hussars.**

In the morning when we were on the top [of Mont Pinçon] *Lieutenant Aldham, my Troop leader – 2nd Troop – told us that we'd lost a company of Wiltshires on the way up. This had been partly because the Germans could direct fire from the top of the Abbey tower, this side of le Plessis Grimoult. We could see it from the top. We then had an artillery shoot on it and had quite a few shots, but without hitting it. Then I said, 'Sir, can I have a go at it? 'He said, if you think you can hit it, have a go.' So I got out, I put cross wires on the barrel, took the striker out and aimed it at the right hand side of the tower. I put the striker back in, got the cross-wires off. I then asked the operator, Montgomery, 'Monty', to put a shell, HE, up the spout – and the first shot the tower went – and all the lads cheering.*

Mme Madeleine Restout:

There was a First Aid post in the building over there; we used to call it the 'Old House'. The father of our first casualty went outside through the shooting to fetch a German doctor The German doctor came to examine the 14-year-old child. 'Is he your son?' he asked 'It is very unfortunate for you because he has been wounded in the stomach and he should be operated on. We have too many of our own wounded to look after. There is no question of our treating civilians. The boy was wounded at 9 o'clock in the morning and died at 4 o'clock that afternoon.

Mme Restaut in 1939.

Chapter Thirteen

Capture of le Plessis Grimoult – 7 August

214 Brigade

On 7 August the scout and carrier platoons of 5 DCLI reconnoitred towards le Plessis Grimoult and the scout platoon met with no opposition until they came to a small hamlet – possibly Crépigny – where they saw 'a party of Germans sunbathing'. When they opened fire on them the Germans were quick to retaliate and counter-attack. Clearly the area was still vigorously held. The Commander 214 Brigade, Brigadier Essame, then made his own reconnaissance with the CO 5 DCLI which he subsequently described in his *History of 43rd Division:*

> *After a dramatic passage through La Varinière, arrived on the hill and crawled forward to a large hole in front of the Worcestershire position. The view ahead was excellent, but only the roofs of the houses of the objective, le Plessis Grimoult, could be seen. The southern slopes of Mont Pinçon, covered in scrub and with a few trees, gave a good line of approach. It was therefore decided that... a real effort should be made to surprise the enemy. The plan decided on was a noisy feint attack down the road which approached le Plessis Grimoult from the west; meanwhile, the bulk of the battalion was to move silently along the lower slopes of Mont Pinçon, then execute a right wheel and attack le Plessis Grimoult from the north. To make room for the DCLI and also to stabilize the ugly situation at the foot of the mountain, 1 Worcestershire, except for one company, were ordered to side-step to the cross-roads at la Varinière.*

A Royal Tiger vanquished by a 2" mortar

1 Worcesters with C Squadron 4/7 Dragoon Guards were to clear up the road to the west of the village, while 5 DCLI with two troops of B Squadron took the village itself. The Worcesters group ran into very heavy mortar fire and had to withdraw. (The remainder of B Squadron was engaged all day with 12 KRRC in a battle round Danvou.) At 2130 hrs, as the light was fading, a heavy bombardment by both guns and mortars began. Behind it the two troops of B Squadron 4/7 Dragoon Guards

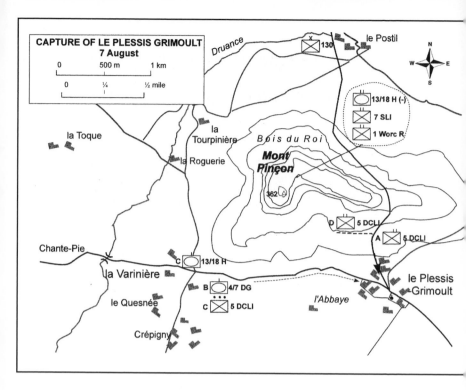

CAPTURE OF LE PLESSIS GRIMOULT
7 August

and a platoon of C Company 5 DCLI advanced on the le Plessis Grimoult from the direction of la Varinière.

Meanwhile A Company of 5 DCLI, followed up by D Company, had moved down the mountain to the northern end of the village after a forced march of four miles. At 1010 A Company, under Major Parker, advanced and quickly disposed of two enemy posts.

Reg Philp was Company Sergeant Major:

We moved down towards Le Plessis Grimoult – it was evening by then – we linked up with the road which runs down the east side of Mont Pinçon. The company and 8 Platoon on the left hand side of the road and I was with company HQ and another platoon on the right hand side of the road. A third platoon was in reserve. There was a bit of cover, no problems, and we did not come up against any Germans until it was getting dark and we came down to the road junction.

As they came into the village they raked houses with their Bren guns and flung in No 36 and No 77 grenades. As the company pushed on the houses behind them were set alight by the phosphorus of the grenades burst into flames. Suddenly they

150

heard tanks ahead and the outline of several vehicles including two Tiger tanks could just be made out. The company PIAT had been knocked out by artillery fire and Major Parker ordered rapid fire at the crossroads – with rifles, Brens and 2" mortars.

Sergeant Major Philp continued:

> To our surprise across the other side of the road against some houses there was a large German tank being loaded with ammunition from a lorry, which was parked right against it. We stopped under cover and watched the Germans, carrying ammunition, smoking cigarettes, talking casually – and they weren't aware we were there! Then a message came to me from the company commander telling me to mortar them. The first HE landed right in the truck it blew up, caught fire and killed the crew; it must have killed them all. The tank also caught fire and exploded from inside. So that was all cleared.

The lorry and one tank burst into flames, throwing up exploding ammunition. The other tank moved off straight away and its crew abandoned the half-track.

Sergeant Fred Bolt was with the 2" mortar:

> We came down the road from Mont Pinçon leading down towards the village. There was a row of trees on the left hand side of the road. I

The village of le Plessis Grimoult after the assault. 'We made our way down, dodging between the houses that were still standing, into the churchyard and hugged the wall of the churchyard as we crept forward.'

was there with the man who fired the 2" mortar. It went up in the air between the trees and dropped right down on the cross roads where the tank was. I thought the bomb went down the turret of the tank and then exploded, but other witnesses say it hit the lorry carrying the ammunition. There was a big bang and then flames came up and that was it.

And Sergeant Major Philp pointed out that the tank that was hit was a Royal Tiger:

62 tons in weight... It was the first Royal Tiger tank to be destroyed in Normandy, a Royal Tiger destroyed by a 2" mortar firing a two-pound bomb! After the tank was destroyed, we moved across the road junction and went into the village proper keeping to the same formation with a platoon on left and right of the road

The company commander and his leading platoon now charged across the crossroads and fought their way through the village to the German headquarters.

We had orders to make as much noise as we could so the Germans would think there were more of us than there really were. [Bolt]

Unfortunately we had to set some of the buildings on fire; the enemy were holding out in them. There were barns full of hay, straw. We cleared the village right through to the far side as we went along. [Philp]

Private James Gregory was in one of the platoons:

We made our way down, dodging between the houses that were still standing, into the churchyard and hugged the wall of the churchyard as we crept forward. Then the NCOs got the order to stay put and hold the perimeter. All the hubbub was over in about twenty, thirty minutes.

After some fighting at close quarters the Germans decided that they had had enough and Major Parker took the surrender of ninety-four prisoners. His own small force was less than forty strong.

The operation was very successful, especially bearing in mind the small number of casualties we had suffered. When we got to the far side of the village we quickly dug shallow trenches to give ourselves some cover against enemy mortar and artillery fire. It was lucky we did this because we were shelled very soon after. [Philp]

Sergeant Bolt had gone into a farm:

There was a big hole in the wall; it was dark but I could hear German voices so I fired a few rounds through the hole. I heard someone scream out – whether I hit someone I'm not certain; I don't think I hit anyone

The *Königstiger* defeated by a 2″ mortar bomb in le Plessis Grimoult.

The King Tiger comes in for some close scrutiny by these British soldiers.

because when they came out of the building no one complained about being hurt, but it certainly frightened them. I think it was a platoon that surrendered – usually about thirty men.

The other two platoons soon arrived and then Lieutenant Colonel Taylor with D Company, followed up by the rest of the battalion. They combed the village and by 2300 hrs any remaining Germans had been killed or taken prisoner. An armoured counter-attack came in soon after dawn, but the DCLI were firmly in possession and had no trouble beating it off. The DCLI could now take stock of their achievement:

With the coming of daylight, the DCLI realized the extent of their astounding success. Thirty-one of the enemy lay dead; 125 prisoners had been taken. A Royal Tiger tank incidentally the first destroyed in Normandy – two Nebelwerfers, one half-track, one staff car and a great deal of miscellaneous equipment had been captured. All this had been achieved at the cost of one man killed, five wounded and one missing.

During the counter-attack, shrapnel from an 88 had caught Major Parker in his jaw and shoulder while a mortar bomb that pitched on a hedge completely buried Sergeant Major Philp:

Fortunately I was not wounded and was only suffering from shock when they pulled me out. Major Parker went back to have his wound treated. However within two days he came back. He had to be in charge of his company. It was his company and couldn't have anyone else doing his job.

The church at le Plessis Grimoult in 2002.

Chapter Fourteen

After the Capture of Mont Pinçon

The Next Few Days

There was no clear-cut end to Operation BLUECOAT for the 'players'. Areas from which the Germans had yet to be cleared had to be 'mopped-up' and then, in quick succession, came the German counter-attack at Mortain, the battle of the 'Falaise pocket' and the advance to the Seine.

During the next few days after the capture of Mont Pinçon many of the units in XXX and VIII Corps continued to be engaged in fierce fighting from which there were further losses in killed and wounded. When possible, units and formations were pulled out for what was often all too brief a rest, during which much needed maintenance of vehicles and equipment could be carried out and small parties of men could enjoy some peace and quiet – and the luxury of baths and cinema shows.

George Formby entertaining the troops.

General Viney:

'One summer evening, I attended a performance of a good concert party led by George Formby, the Lancashire comedian and banjo player, which went on until about dark. Formby told me it was their tenth performance that day and they had been on the go since early in the morning.'

Lieutenant General Brian Horrocks.

The XXX Corps Commander, General Horrocks, quickly made personal use of Mont Pinçon as a vantage point and set up an OP for himself, to which his divisional commanders would be summoned. General Verney found reaching the OP to be an unpleasant affair:

A more unpleasant drive it would be hard to imagine. The road up was frequently shelled and it was considered wise to park the cars on the reverse slope and then run to reach the pit. General Horrocks was one of those rare people who was stimulated by being shelled, rather as some are stimulated by a good gallop. It was nice for him being made like that but no fun for his companions.

During the battle south of Mont Pinçon on 9 August, RHQ of 13/18 Hussars:

... were sitting up behind the mountain – and certainly got our fair share of stonk – some very near ones when we thought we were cunningly placed, sitting under a sharp ridge where they should have gone over our heads but didn't.

Later we moved on to the top and had a look at the battle. A perfectly tremendous view and we could easily see the 7th Armoured Division battle ... We weren't shelled here much but a bloody 88mm. gun potted at us intermittently. We sat there some time and enjoyed the view.

While all this was going on, General Thomas (known as 'von Thoma'), G.O.C. 43 Division, came wandering over the hill by himself. He saw me and came across – he has the reputation of being a frightful fire-eater, but after last week's efforts he looked at the badge and let out a beaming smile, saying how delighted he was to see us again, how sorry he was we had to leave him and how he had enjoyed and appreciated our support last week. (Neave)

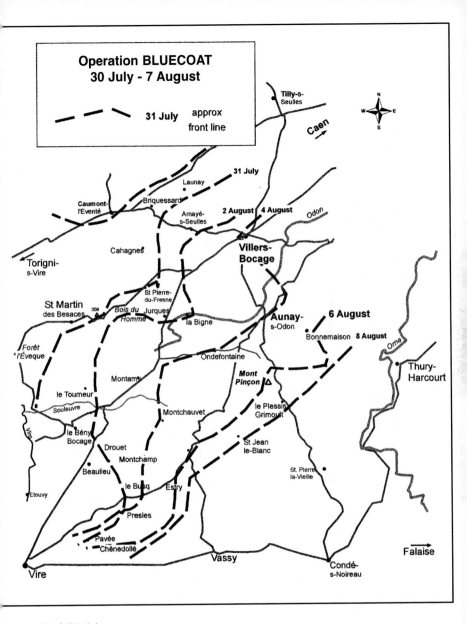

Operation BLUECOAT
30 July - 7 August

– – – – **31 July**   approx front line

Tilly-s-Seulles

Caen

Launay

31 July

Caumont-l'Eventé

Briquessard

Amayé-s-Seulles

2 August   4 August

Odon

Cahagnes

Villers-Bocage

Torigni-s-Vire

St Pierre-du-Fresne

St Martin des Besaces

309

Bois du Homme

Jurques

la Bigne

Aunay-s-Odon

6 August

Bonnemaison   **8 August**

Orne

Forêt l'Éveque

Ondefontaine

Thury-Harcourt

Montam?

Mont Pinçon △

le Toumeur

Souleuvre

Montchauvet

le Plessis Grimoult

Vire

le Bény Bocage

Drouet

Montchamp

St Jean le-Blanc

St. Pierre la-Vieille

Beaulieu

le Busq

Estry

Etouvy

Presles

Pavée

Chênedollé

Vassy

Condé-s-Noireau

Falaise

Vire

43rd Division

Early on 8 August, 4 Dorsets arrived in the area of la Ferrière - Duval-Chante Pie, and prepared to meet an enemy counterattack. That did not materialise but they remained in their position throughout the next day, patrolling vigorously despite the blistering heat.

> *'La Varinière cross-roads had now acquired an evil reputation only comparable with that of Hell Fire Corner on the Menin Road at Ypres in the first war.'* [Essame]

On 8 August it was still cut off from le Plessis Grimoult by enemy immediately south of the road and mortar and machine-gun fire from them and from the villages of le Quesnée and Crépigny, continued throughout the day. 1 Worcestershire with a squadron from 4/7 Dragoon Guards was given the task of cleaning up which took two more days of fierce fighting, during which the squadron leader of the 4th/7th was killed. The Divisional Reconnaissance Regiment, who had been holding a position just south-west of the strongly-held St Jean le Blanc, could at last seize that village.

By the following morning all the high ground dominating the Druance had been secured by 214 Brigade. The brigade remained on Mont Pinçon, under heavy shelling and mortaring and, next day, continued mopping in support of 50th Division's advance, while 130 Brigade cleared the woods south of Chante Pie.

8 Armoured Brigade

4/7 Dragoon Guards, less the squadron with the Worcesters, took part in the 50th Division advance, as did the 13th/18th. The latter and the Sherwood Rangers had been promised two to four days rest, but the 13th/18th were soon disillusioned, as Julius Neave noted in his diary for the 8th:

> *On return to harbour we settled down for a quiet night and took off our boots and hoped they would leave us alone.*
>
> *Everyone was really pretty whacked, we hadn't had our boots off for three nights – but no sooner had we settled in than on the air comes the Brigadier saying we are to go off and support the 50 Division in an attack tomorrow. Bloody annoying, and most irritating after all our promises – but there it is – we have lost a number of tanks so they will be short of them and they have had no maintenance for over 10 days.*

50th Division

50th Division, now back from their short rest, advanced through 43rd Division, with support from 8 Armoured Brigade.

7th Armoured Division

The Corps-plan on 8 August was for two columns of tanks

158

13th/18th Hussars tank crew catching up on rest and writing letters home.

and infantry from 7th Armoured Division to advance on Condé, over ten miles away. Neither column got started: 'As soon as they began to advance on the top of the plateau they met stiff opposition, and the country was too thick for tanks.' However, by the evening of the 9th they had cleared the crest by Mont Pinçon and la Vallée. Then the bulk of the division was taken out of the line for two week's rest.

15th Division

Estry was still being defended vigorously on 7 August and 15th Division suffered severe casualties while establishing itself in the northern outskirts. The Germans did not intend to withdraw without a bitter struggle and the Corps Commander decided that the two armoured divisions should hold the line in the centre of the Corps' front, while the infantry on either side exerted pressure on the enemy.

The fighting is over... for a little while.

Guards Armoured Division

Guards Armoured enjoyed 'forty-eight hours of comparative rest', but soon the division was required to take over much of the 11th Armoured Division frontage while they were taken out in preparation for a new role.

11th Armoured Division

Across the whole BLUECOAT area, most of the towns and village were little more than shambles. In the 11th Division sector, this was particularly so of such places as Chênedollé, Presles, Burcy, Pavée, le Bas Perrier, le Moulin and le Grand Bonfaits – all of which had had the awfulness of war brought suddenly amongst them. 'It was a good harvest that August of 1944. The corn stood high, there were cows to milk and livestock to feed. Many civilians had abandoned homes and taken to roads with their pathetic possessions. Wheelbarrows, prams, small carts, little groups trying to avoid fighting, some on bicycles. Always very old or very young.'

A Month Later

Each evening, after the 9 o'clock news, the well-known broadcaster John Snagge presented the day's 'War Report' on the BBC Home Service. On 7 September, four weeks after the capture of Mont Pinçon, Snagge introduced: 'a personal story ... it is the story of a British Commander – Lieutenant General B.G. Horrocks, CB, DSO, MC – and it is told by Chester Wilmot.'

Barely eight weeks ago Lieutenant General B. G. Horrocks who commanded the leading British troops in the advance from the Seine to Antwerp was lying in a convalescent home in Britain. For more than a year he had been in hospital. In fact ever since a machine gun bullet had gone through his shoulder and down his leg in Bizerta in May 1943. He'd had six major operations and the doctors said he could never return to an active position. But as General Horrocks himself said, this was no time to be lying around in a convalescent home; and when General Montgomery, as he was then, asked him to take command of' a corps in France, General Horrocks could not get there quickly enough. That was early in August, and the return to a fighting command was the tonic he needed. He galvanised his corps into action, punched it through to Mont Pinçon and the Orne, and helped to clean up the Falaise pocket. Within a few weeks his tall, lithe figure, his angular features, his ready friendly smile and his restless energy were well known to his forward troops. He was always up with them. Field Marshal Montgomery could not have found a better man for the job of' chasing the Germans out of Northern France. Horrocks has done this kind of thing before – in Tunis. and as he himself said yesterday, I'm a very good General when they're running away – I like motoring better than fighting. – That is true, but; it is Horrocks who makes them run.

Next night John Snagge followed up with:

Here is a great story ... one of the greatest of this War. It is the story of the fighting advance of one British corps from Normandy to Brussels and it was told to Matthew Halton of C.B.C. by the General who commands it. Here is Halton's despatch:

The man who commands that corps took time off today to come to a hotel in Brussels and tell war correspondents about his battle. He is a grey-haired, gentle, amiable man, with a Roman nose – but he is one of the great soldiers of the war. ...First, he took us back to Mont Pinçon in Normandy. That high ground south of Villers Bocage was to the British what the road from Caen to Falaise was to the Canadians. That is what it was; a bloody hellhole where men gasped and fought day after day, day after day for every foot o' ground – but a hellhole where the guts

161

were torn out of the German Army. The General told us how one British division took Mont Pinçon in twenty-four hours. He said: "It was a brilliant attack by exhausted men. There was the bitterest fighting I have ever seen. And what really made it possible was the work of six tanks. Six tanks, no more, made a wild dash into the enemy and got up on top of' the hill and stayed there fighting in the middle of the Germans. They sent a message back: "We are lonely but we are all right". That was the climax of the Battle of Normandy. But there was still hard fighting all the way from Mont Pinçon to the Seine.

Major Lord Methuen had landed in Normandy on 27 August as a 'Monuments, Fine Arts & Archives Officer' for 21st Army Group. He was an early visitor to le Plessis Grimoult.

9th Sept. CAEN to BAYEUX to confer with Monsieur Leroy about first-aid to buildings under his care . . . I then took the truck and went south into the schist [a type of chrystattine rock] country called the Bocage, where villages tend to thin out and grass and apple orchards predominate. It is not a rich country compared to the plain, but an undulating one and rising to some height at LE PLESSIS GRIMOULT (MT PINÇON). The village has been much shot up, as there was heavy fighting here. The former priory (monument inscrit) has been damaged. Part of this building was a ruin and part inhabited. The west tower, with its gothic entrance, has not suffered but the adjoining building has had its roof holed; the interesting long dwelling-house at right angles to it with its pointed doorways has suffered much from shell-bursts and has been scarred by bullets; the roof and walls on one side have been badly holed.

In 1996 a memorial on the summit of Mont Piçon was dedicated to those who served in the 13/18 Royal Hussars between 1922 and 1992. Visitors to the memorial in 2002.

Battle Honours

'Mont Pincon 30th July to 9th August, 1944' was amongst the Second World War battle honours awarded in 1957. *'VIII, XII and XXX Corps took part in this Battle. It covered the operations leading up to the capture of Mont Pincon, following the American break-out in the west.'* The Honour was emblazoned (shown on colours, standards and guidons) by the:

4th/7th Dragoon Guards	Royal Warwickshire Regiment
5th Dragoon Guards	Somerset Light Infantry
13th/18th Hussars	Gloucestershire Regiment
Northamptonshire Yeomanry	Worcestershire Regiment
Grenadier Guards	Duke of Cornwall's Light Infantry
Coldstream Guards	Middlesex Regiment
Irish Guards	Wiltshire Regiment
Welsh Guards	Queen's Westminsters

and was also awarded to the:

Life Guards	Cameronians
Royal Horse Guards	Royal Hampshire Regiment
8th Hussars	Dorset Regiment
11th Hussars	King's Shropshire Light Infantry
Royal Tank Regiment	King's Royal Rifle Corps
Sherwood Rangers Yeomanry	North Staffordshire Regiment
Scots Guards	Highland Light Infantry
Royal Scots	Seaforth Highlanders
Queen's Royal Regiment	Argyll and Sutherland Highlanders
East Yorkshire Regiment	Rifle Brigade
Royal Scots Fusiliers	London Rifle Brigade
Cheshire Regiment	Monmouthshire Regiment
King's Own Scottish Borderers	Herefordshire Light Infantry

Honours were also awarded for the 'subsidiary engagements' at:

'Quarry Hill' 30 July to 2 August *'15th Division with 6th Guards Tank Brigade under command secured 'Quarry Hill' (Point 309 to the west of the Bois du Homme) with 4 Tank Coldstream Guards, Glasgow Highlanders and 7 Seaforth. The position was firmly held during ensuing days.'*

'Jurques' 30 July to 4 August *'43rd Division, advancing to the Bois du Homme, ran into stubborn resistance near Bricquessard. Progress was made in face of stiff opposition about Cahagnes and St Pierre-du-Fresne, Jurques being captured on 2nd August.'*

'La Variniere' 4 to 9 August *'43rd Division and 8th Armoured Brigade advancing eastwards reached La Variniere on 6th August. Here 5 Wiltshires found a strongly posted enemy. By that evening 13/18 Hussars followed by 4 Wiltshires had reached the crest of Mont Pincon – Point 361. 5/DCLI cleared Le Plessis Grimoult, and stiff fighting continued on 8th and 9th August, about Le Quesnee and Les Hameaux.'*

'Souleuvre' 30 July to 1 August *'The operations by 11th Armoured and Guards Armoured Divisions south of Caumont led to the capture of St Martin-des-Besaces, whilst the crossing of the River Souleuvre by 2 Household Cavalry Regiment and 2 Northamptonshire Yeomanry led to the capture of Le Beny Bocage.'*

'Catheolles' 2 to 5 August *'covered fighting by Guards Armoured Division and 15th Division against stubborn resistance.'*

'Le Perier Ridge' 2 to 8 August *'11th Armoured Division, advancing beyond the Souleuvre, was halted on the Vire-Vassy road and withdrew to Le Perier Ridge. Here, with 3rd Division, they defeated enemy counter-attacks with tanks and infantry.'*

History of 43rd Division

The capture of Mont Pinçon will go down to history as a very great feat of arms ... All ranks of all units of the service within the Division and 8 Armoured Brigade share the honour. It is fitting, however, in conclusion to pay especial tribute to the three main fighting arms in their traditional order – to the Cavalry represented by 8 Armoured Brigade, who brought a new spirit into the division's battles and whose tanks were the first to gain the crest; to the Royal Artillery, whose devastating, accurate and unfailing support time and time again saved the day; and finally to the endurance, courage and fighting skill of the Infantry. Above all shines the great sacrifice of Lieutenant Colonel Pearson and the pitifully few survivors of 5th Wiltshire Regiment, who at the crisis of the battle finally carried the cross-roads at La Varinière and turned the tide. (History of 43rd Division)

Chapter Fifteen

Visitor's Guide to Mont Pinçon

Touring the BLUECOAT area

Travel to Normandy

Most visitors to the Normandy battlefields travel by car. However, with the area's proximity to ports, a number of hardy souls are cycling around the battlefields. Anyone whose journey starts in the UK has to get across or under the Channel. The nearest ferry service to the area of Operation BLUECOAT is the Brittany Ferries route from Portsmouth to Ouistreham, which is less than twenty minutes drive from Caen and is alongside Sword Beach. Further away, one hour thirty minutes drive to the west, is Cherbourg, which is served by sailings from Portsmouth, Southampton and Poole. Equidistant but to the east is le Havre, served by ferries from Portsmouth and Southampton. Choice for most visitors depends on the convenience of the sailing times and, of course, relative costs. Do not forget special offers. To the east of Normandy are the shorter, and consequently cheaper, crossings in the Boulogne and Calais area. For those who dislike ferries there is the Channel Tunnel, but this option, though quicker, is usually more expensive. From the Calais area, Normandy can be easily reached via the new autoroutes in less than four hours, but bear in mind toll charges. (They can be reduced by avoiding the Pont de Normandie.)

Maps

Good maps are an essential prerequisite to a successful battlefield visit. Best of all is a combination of contemporary and modem maps. The *Battleground Series* of course, provides a variety of maps. However, a full map sheet enables the visitor or indeed those who are exploring the battlefield from the comfort of their armchair, to put the battle in a wider context. A number of modern map series are available in both the UK and Normandy. Most readily available in both countries are the Michelin 1:200,000 Yellow Series. Sheet 54 covers the British and US D-Day, build-up and break-out battle areas and is useful for getting around the Normandy battlefields and ports. Better still are the *Institut Geographique National (IGN) 1:100,000 Série Verte* (Green Series) maps. Sheets 6 and 17 cover the Normandy battle area. The *Série Verte* maps have the advantage of showing contours and other details such as unmade roads and tracks. The most detailed maps, readily available in France, can also be obtained from

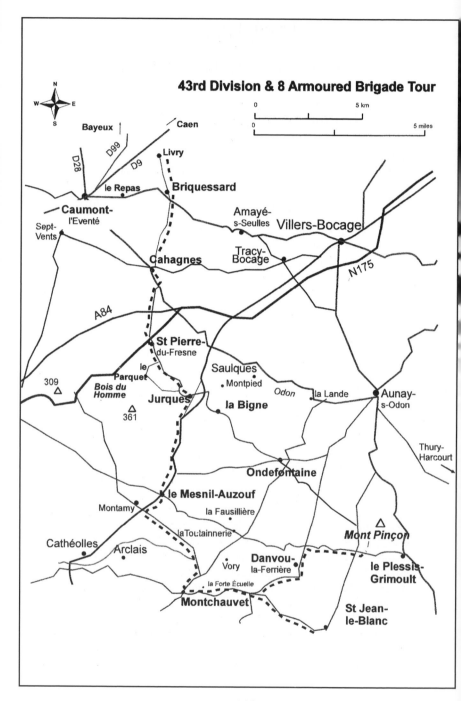

43rd Division & 8 Armoured Brigade Tour

specialist shops such as Stanfords in London (www.stanfords.co.uk) or by special order from high street bookshops. They are the *IGN Série Bleue* in 1:25,000 scale. The complete area of BLUECOAT requires four sheets: 1413 E Caumont l'Éventé 15 13E Aunay-s-Odon, Villers-Bocage; 1414 E Vire; 1514 O Condé-s-Noireau.

Place Names

The names of places in the different accounts of BLUECOAT actions are sometimes a touch difficult to reconcile with those on present day maps. Partly that can be accounted for by errors in such sources as formation and unit war diaries, often compiled in haste by weary men with their minds half on the next operation, rather than the last. There are also differences in the maps used. Notably, most accounts, and contemporary maps, of the operations of July and August 1944 refer to a village called 'Montcharivel'. That is also known as 'Montchauvet' – and that is how it appears on modern maps and is how I have rendered it. But there also differences between modern maps, eg some refer to the Bois du Homme, others to Bois de Brimbois. But then part of the fascination of finding one's way over old battlegrounds is the detective work involved!

'l'Affrontement'

Operation BLUECOAT took place over a wide area and anyone wishing to obtain a general 'feel' of the country involved – and who has not previously visited this part of Normandy – could well make use of the whole or part of the itinerary marked by the Normandy tourist organisation: 'l'Affrontement' ('Confrontation'). That is one of eight routes, signposted 'Normandie Terre-Liberté, marking phases of the Battle of Normandy. (The others are: Overlord- l'Assaut, D Day-le Choc, Objectif-un Port, Cobra-la Percée, la Contre-Attaque, l'Encerclement, le Dénouement.) Each site along a route is marked with a *totem* giving a brief (and not always accurate!) description of the action that took place there. 'l'Affrontement' is particularly convenient for those arriving by ferry at Ouistreham – the port for Caen. Its sites are listed below with those of particular relevance to BLUECOAT shown in bold type:

1. Pegasus Bridge
2. Site de Lébisey
3. Mémorial par la Paix à Caen
4. Site d'Authie
5. Site de Carpiquet
6. Site de St Manvieu-Norrey
7. Site de Bretteville-l'Orgueilleuse
8. Site de Cheux
9. Site du Pont Tourmanville

10. Site de la Côte 112
11. Site d'Evrecy
12. Site de Villers-Bocage
13. Fontenay-le-Pesnil
14. Musée de la Bataille de Tilly-sur-Seulles
15. Site de Hottot-les-Bagues
16. Site de Caumont-l'Eventé
17. **Musée de Saint Martin-des-Besaces**
18. **Site de Pont de Taureau**
19. **Site de Bény-Bocage**
20. **Cimetière Britannique de Saint Charles-de-Percy**
21, **Site de Vire**
22. **Mont Pinçon** [in le Plessis-Grimoult]
23. **Site de Aunay-sur-Odon**

43rd Division and 8 Armoured Brigade Tour (see Map)

However, this book has concentrated on the actions in which units of 43rd Division and 8 Armoured Brigade were involved and a route is suggested below which follows in their tracks.

Via Bayeux

A useful preliminary would be a visit to the Musée Mémorial de la Bataille de Normandie at Bayeux. The layout of pictures and maps follows a roughly chronological order in which Operation BLUECOAT is included. But the main value is in the extensive range of exhibits – armoured and 'soft' vehicles, artillery and other weapons – many of which are referred to in the text. (The rest areas of 43rd Division and 8 Armoured Brigade, prior to BLUECOAT were south-east of Bayeux, around Condé-s-Seulles, Chouain, Ducy-Ste-Marguerite, Coulombs.)

From Bayeux take the D572 towards St Lô for 6 km and turn left on D99. That takes you to the assembly areas of the 43rd Division brigades, on the reverse slopes of the ridge running north-east from Caumont-l'Eventé. 129 Brigade was in and around la Mirrerie, a kilometre north of Livry; 214 Brigade in the area la Paumerie, north-west of Livry; 130 Brigade between Couvigny and le Repas, between Livry and Caumont.

Via Caen

However, if you are arriving via Caen, take the N13 towards Bayeux and, at the Carpiquet turnoff, take the D9 for Caumont-l'Eventé. Further along this road, after the turn off to Tilly-sur-Seulles, are le Lion Vert and la Croix des Landes, from which the 50th Division advance began. The D9 was the start line for them and for 43rd Division. In about 13 km is a turning left on D115 to Livry and Briquessard.

Briquessard, Cahagnes and St Pierre-du-Fresne (see Chapter 2)

To follow 130 Brigade attack towards Briquessard take the road out of Livry and over the ridge, down into **Briquessard** and on to **Cahagnes** (D292). (If you are using the large scale map 1413 E you could follow the right flanking advance, taken by 7 Hampshire.) From Cahagnes, a short distance south along the D54, there is a turning right, D291, which takes you to les Haies Tigard (across the A84 which is, of course, a post-war creation) and **St Pierre-du-Fresne**.

Bois du Homme, Jurques and la Bigne (see Chapter 4)

Confusedly, Bois du Homme and Point 361 appear on some maps; on others they are Bois de Brimbois and Point 358! There are various tracks up the hill, but in 1944 the approach appears to have been from the road which turns left off N175, towards le Parquet. However the main thrust of the division was on Jurques, la Bigne – and Ondefontaine. The road left from le Parquet takes you on to **Jurques**. Or, if you turn off the N175 at **les Haies Tigard** the D291 also leads to Jurques, which nowadays is by-passed by the main road to Vire (D577). From Jurques if you stay on D291 (going under the D577) you come to **la Bigne** -

Ondefontaine (see Chapter 6)

And can continue on D291 to **Ondefontaine**. Glimpses of Mont Pinçon may now be seen – in fine weather – easily distinguished by the vast, red and white striped, radio/TV mast (*centrémetteur de radio et TV du Mont Pinçon*) sited on the eastern edge of the feature. From Ondefontaine, roads radiate to several of the places mentioned in the text: D114 to le Mesnil-Auzouf; D290 to la Tautainerie and Montchauvet; D114/D26 to Aunay-s-Odon.

le Mesnil-Auzouf and Montchauvet

But, again, the division's main thrust was via le Mesnil-Auzouf. For ease of following the course of events, it is probably best to head straight there from Jurques on D 577 and turn off it, into the village of **le Mesnil-Auzouf** and left onto the road towards Danvou – D165. This was the 'northern' of the two routes initially taken by 129 Brigade, but it is difficult to tell which was which as the 'southern' is said to have 'petered out'. It is best to head for **Montchauvet** and then take D298 towards St Jean-le-Blanc. (If you are using the 1:25,000 maps you are now struggling with the junction of the four sheets!) La Forte Êcuelle is where the leading column came under fire and halted for the night.

'Converging on Mont Pinçon' (see Chapter 8)

D298 joins briefly D26, the road from Vire to Aunay, but where that turns left, keeps on to St Jean-le-Blanc. In about 2km the road bends through trees and in the dip is the bridge over the Druance that replaces the one which 4 Wilts found blown. In another km is St Jean-le-Blanc itself.

There is a road from St Jean-le-Blanc to la Varinière (via **le Quesnée**), but it would be preferable to return to the D26 and turn towards Aunay. That takes you through Danvou-la-Ferrière to a junction with D16 – towards le Plessis Grimoult. Turn right on to D165; you are now on the approach which 5 Wilts took, and **Chante-Pie** is a short distance ahead. Continue along the road – it goes down into a dip and across the Druance, but a bridge as such no longer exists.

Gaining a Footing and The Assault (see Chapters 9 and 10 and maps on pp 108 & 120)

From this point it would be easiest to stay with 5 Wilts and A Squadron 13/18 Hussars and continue along D165 towards la Varinière and le Plessis Grimoult. That takes you to the crossroads with D106 – heading north to and south to le Quesnée. From what had been the bridge up to this crossroads and beyond is the area that was so bitterly fought over on 6 August. (See maps on pp 108 and 120.)

Continue over the crossroads towards le Plessis Grimoult and in a short distance there is a sign pointing to the left for the **13th/18th Royal Hussars (QMO) Memorial Mont Pinçon**. The turning may be the one leading on to the track that the two troops of tanks took in 1944, but what is now a made up road does not follow the track itself – that twisted and turned much more. Pat Hennessey, who frequently revisited the site since then, could not himself be sure which track it was that they took! (Personally, I think it may be one that turns off the main track to the left, not far from the main road. That goes up by an old quarry which may be where Sergeant Rattle's tank slithered.) However, if you stay on the main track, when you get to the memorial, that is the rough area where they leaguered and from it you can see – if you are there on 'a lovely summer evening' – the vista which Noel Denny described.

A memorial was dedicated, on 6 August 1996, to all those who served in the 13/18 Hussars from 1922 to 1992. On the gate to the footpath leading down to it, plaques in French and English commemorate the people of the local communes, who suffered in the battles for the Liberation of France. On top of the memorial proper (constructed in Brittany granite) is a panorama depicting the situation at approximately 1800 hrs on 6 August 1944, as the two troops of tanks came up the track.

There is the same difficulty in identifying tracks if you look for the area of the **4 Som LI** attack or the route taken by **B Squadron 13/18 Hussars** through the fog. However, if you retrace your steps to the D106, turn right along it to **la Roguerie**. From there you can see how exposed were the infantry trying to advance up the steep slope of the hill. The road continues to a junction with D54 (Aunay-le Plessis Grimoult) and about half way along, looking to the left, is the country across which 7 Hampshire led the feint attack. Their first objective, **le Plecière**, is not shown on most maps, but is down in the valley of the Druance stream.

Night on Mont Pinçon (Chapter 12)

From the **13th/18th Memorial** the road across Mont Pinçon takes you eventually to the Aunay-le Plessis Grimoult road (D54) and the base of the radio/TV mast. (Near it is another sign to the memorial.) En route you can obtain a good impression of the ground that the British and German troops 'shared' during the night of 6/7 August. At the highest point, 362, there is now a pictorial panoramic view – its value somewhat diminished by the surrounding bushes.

Capture of le Plessis Grimoult (Chapter 13 and map on p150)

Turn right down the road to le Plessis Grimoult and, as you near the village, you join the route taken by A Company 5 DCLI. Continue into the village and the churchyard backs on to one corner of the square, surrounded by the wall alongside which men of the DCLI crept during their attack. On the opposite corner is the *totem* erected on the route *l'Affrontement*. Nearby is a plaque (placed there in 1997):

This plaque is to commemorate the liberation of LE PLESSIS GRIMOULT on August 7th 1944 by the 5th Bn. THE DUKE OF CORNWALL'S LIGHT INFANTRY supported by   the 43rd Division.

(They seem to have forgotten 8 Armoured Brigade and 4/7 DG!)

Bibliography

BS Barnes *The Sign Of The Double 'T' (The 50th Northumbrian Division – July 1943 to December 1944)* (Sentinel Press 1999)

J Brissard *The Charge of the Bull. 11th Armoured Division in Normandy 1944* (Batus Books 1989)

JM Brereton *History of the 4th/7th Royal Dragoon Guards 1685-1980* (Regiment 1982)

D S Daniell *The Hampshire Regiment Vol 3 1918-1954* (Gale & Polden 1955)

P Delaforce *The Black Bull – from Normandy to the Baltic with 11th Armoured Division* (Alan Sutton Publishing 1993)

P Delaforce, *The Fighting Wessex Wyverns* (Alan Sutton Publishing, 1994)

H. Essame *The 43rd Wessex Division at War 1944-5* (W Clowes 1952)

P Forbes *6th Guards Tank Brigade – The Story of Guardsmen in Churchill Tanks* (Sampson Low)

EG Godfrey *The Duke of Cornwall's Light Infantry,* (Images Publishing [Malvern] Ltd, 1994)

*P Hennessey, Young Man in a Tank (Privately published 1988)

B Horrocks, (with E Belfield and H Essame), *Corps Commander* (Sidgwick & Jackson 1977)

S Jary *18 Platoon,* (Sydney Jary Ltd 1987)

JS McMath *5th Battalion Wiltshire Regiment In N W Europe June 1944 – May 1945* (Whitefriars)

HG Martin The *History Of The Fifteenth Scottish Division 1939-1945* (William Blackwood, 1948)

Methuen, Lord, *Normandy Diary* (Robert Hale, 1952)

CH Miller *History of the 13th/18th Royal Hussars (Q.M.O.) 1922-47* (Chisman, Bradshaw 1949)

Field Marshal Montgomery *Memoirs* (Hutchinson)

Field Marshal Montgomery *Normandy to the Baltic* (Hutchinson 1947)

R Neillands *The Desert Rats 7th Armoured Division 1940-45* (Weidenfeld & Nicolson 1991)

Rosse, Earl of & ER Hill *The Story of the Guards Armoured Division* (Geoffrey Bles 1956)

GL Verney *The Desert Rats. The History of the 7th Armoured Division 1938 to 1945* (Hutchinson)

War Office Battle Honours Committee 1958 *Battle Honours of the Second World War 1939-45*

GJB Watkins *From Normandy to the Weser (4th Bn. Dorset Regiment 1944-1945)* (Dorset Press)

P Whately-Smith *94th (Dorset & Hants) Fd. Regiment Royal Artillery 1939-1945* (Dorset Press)

C Wilmot, *Struggle for Europe* (Collins, 1952)

Diaries

War Diaries of: 13/18 Hussars; Sherwood Rangers Yeomanry

*JAS Neave The War Diary of Julius Neave (Privately published 1995)

Diary of A Sqn 13/18H 1944-45, edited by Major General DB Wormald, 1990 (13th/18th Hussars Museum typescript)

Diary of C Sqn 13/18H 1944-45 (13th/18th Hussars Museum typescript)

Audio-Visual

**AAG Productions *Battle for Mont Pinçon 5th, 6th and 7th August 1944* (75 mins) Audio-recorded interview with Major RAM Neave, 1991. 13th/18th Hussars Museum

* Copies from Home HQ, The Light Dragoons, Fenham Barracks, Newcastle upon Tyne NE2 4NP)

INDEX

173